PATHWISE® Data-Driven School Improvement Series

Creating a Process

Peter J. Holly

Educational Testing Service

Educational Testing Service
MS 18-D
Rosedale Road
Princeton, NJ 08541-0001
Web site: http://www.ets.org/pathwise

ISBN 0-88685-244-7

Printed in the United States of America

07 06 05 04 03 02   10 9 8 7 6 5 4 3 2 1

Table of Contents

INTRODUCTION

Creating a Process is the second workbook in the PATHWISE® *Data-Driven School Improvement Series. Creating a Process* focuses on data-driven continuous improvement in schools and, specifically, the role of data-based decision making within the process of school improvement planning and implementation. This workbook is for educators who wish to commit to data-based decision making for continuous school improvement.

Data use and shared decision making are not ends in themselves; they are the connected means to ends that really matter—school improvement for enhanced student achievement. How this is all done constitutes a new and more educator-friendly way of generating change in education. What is also different about this workbook series is that it is both an invitation to participate in the change process and, in terms of the practical exercises and tasks included, an ongoing set of supports for those who accept the invitation. The series of workbooks is designed for Learning Teams and Study Groups ("Change Circles") with opportunities for individual reflection built into the collaborative process. However, each workbook can also be useful for individual educators, who would then be encouraged to share their reflective work with immediate colleagues, and for a whole school faculty, working in small groups and coming together to share ideas and make decisions.

Other workbooks in this series will cover such related topics as follows:

- data processing

- classroom action research

- leadership for continuous improvement

GROUP PROCESS GUIDE

The PATHWISE: *Data-Driven School Improvement Series* is a set of tools designed to assist teams of teachers and administrators in the process of school improvement. Although an individual wishing to improve the teaching and learning in a single classroom could undertake many of the activities, the activities are generally presented in the context of group work. The workbooks are sequential in moving through the school improvement process, and the activities are sequential within each workbook. Each activity is designed to build upon those that precede it and to add to the groundwork for those that follow. This **Group Process Guide** is provided to assist facilitators and team members in making the activities effective in achieving their intended purposes. In some instances the activities are intended to help teams identify areas for school improvement focus; other activities are meant to help the team members hone their skills in the group process.

The completion of activities by a school improvement team (referred to in this text as a Learning Team) should reflect the style and needs of that unique team. For a variety of reasons, different teams will move through the tasks with different time requirements and differing levels of commitment to the specific tasks. Some teams who use the materials may be coming together for the first time; others may be long existing and well functioning prior to using these materials as a guide in the school improvement process. It is important to allow your team to use the activities provided to assist your work, but allow your own style to influence how you accomplish each task.

Stages of Group Development

A brief discussion of the stages of groups may assist teams in identifying their level of development. When a team first begins its work together, it is in the **Forming** stage. At this stage the leader/facilitator must take a strong role as the group is still dependent on the leader for guidance and direction. The team's questions focus on the clarity of the task. The behavior of the team is usually polite, impersonal, and sometimes, guarded. Scott Peck (1987), in his discussion of the stages of community making, has labeled this stage "pseudocommunity." He issues a caution for groups in this stage—there is a tendency to fake it by avoiding any conflict and "being extremely pleasant with one another" (p. 86). School improvement teams should use this polite phase to agree on the task at hand and the ground rules that will guide their work as each task inevitably becomes more challenging.

School teams who are grappling with difficult school improvement issues will, quite naturally, move to the next stage of development—**Storming**. This stage also requires the skill of an effective facilitator along with group process techniques to move effectively through the stage. Peck (1987) aptly calls this stage "chaos" as the inevitable conflicts among members become apparent. Part of the storming aspect of this stage can be attributed to the tendency of team members to attempt to convert others to their way of thinking. A challenge for the facilitator and team members in this stage is to be aware that confrontations in this stage tend to be confronting people, rather than issues. The ground rules agreed upon in the **Forming** stage become useful and necessary at this stage. The chaos that the team feels at this stage is not counterproductive; confronting the differing ideas in the group increases the understanding of each other among the team members. It also allows them to examine the strength that each differing opinion brings to their team's effectiveness.

It is this understanding of their diversity that assists groups in moving to the third stage—**Norming**. As individual team members come to feel understood by the others and come to appreciate the strengths in their colleagues, they are able to "empty" (Peck, 1987) the need to convert others to their way and replace that need with a commitment to finding the collective good for the school. During the **Norming** stage, groups are developing the skill to make group decisions. Procedures for group work become routine and expected. The team is able to give and receive feedback and to confront issues rather than individuals. For many teams, this phase happens so quickly and easily, in comparison to the **Storming** phase, that they find themselves in the fourth stage without recognizing the third.

Stage Four is **Performing**—or "community" in Scott Peck's (1987) terms. At this point the team has matured into a closeness; they are "in community" with one another. Teams that have achieved this level of effectiveness are resourceful, flexible, open, and supportive. They are able to accomplish difficult tasks and make challenging decisions. They share ideas and strategies while respecting the gifts of other team members.

The purpose of including this overview of group development in this **Group Process Guide** is twofold. First, it is important that teams understand that *all* groups go through these stages of development to get to the point where they can function most effectively and efficiently. Groups should, therefore, anticipate these stages and not be surprised by the group experiences in each stage. Second, there is a caution about Stage Two—**Storming**. Because *all* groups must go through these stages, the storming cannot be avoided if a team truly desires to become a "performing" team. It is possible to retreat back into the politeness of pseudocommunity, but the team will not function as well or achieve as much if the members are unwilling to do the hard work of becoming a highly functioning team.

Group Process Techniques

Ground Rules

Facilitators and team members can take advantage of a variety of group process techniques to assist them in moving through their development and thereby, ensure that they accomplish their intended purpose—to improve their schools. Most of these strategies and techniques are like the paddles of a war canoe and used only when appropriate and necessary. However, the foundation for all strategies, and therefore necessary at all times, are GROUND RULES (sometimes referred to as norms or group behavior expectations.) Examples of ground rules are as follows:

- Seek opportunities to be involved.

- Praise others, no putdowns.

- Seek to understand, then to be understood (active listening).

- Include all members (a community feeling).

- Empathize—put yourself in another's place.

- Offer the right to pass.

- Ensure confidentiality—what is said in the group, stays in the group.

Groups should establish the ground rules that enable them to work together respectfully in all phases of development. It is the ground rules that assist a group in working through the storming phase while maintaining the integrity of the group's work.

The Foundational Layer of Teamwork Skills

As stated previously, group process strategies will be selected and implemented throughout this workbook depending on the activity to be accomplished. The following list of basic strategies, introduced in the first workbook, *Conceptualizing a New Path*, while an attempt to be comprehensive, is not exclusive. Facilitators and team members are encouraged to use other foundational strategies that they have found to be effective in the school improvement planning process. There are excellent resource materials available that provide further ideas (see, in particular, Johnson and Johnson, 2000, and Garmston and Wellman, 1999). The strategies included below, however, are the ones that will be referenced and utilized in the activities in this workbook.

Circle Configuration

The physical arrangement for the team when working should be as close to a circle as possible. Each member of the group should be able to easily hear all others when they speak. The facilitator should sit (not stand) in the circle. All members of the team have an equal voice and equal responsibility for the success of the team.

Groupings

In order to provide team members with the opportunity to reflect and clarify their own thinking as well as to understand that of the other team members, a variety of groupings within the team should be used during activities. At times, individuals should reflect on their own. Dyads (pairs) should be used to allow all members to share their ideas in the safety of a single partnership. Triads (groups of three) can be used for the same purpose. At times it is very effective to reflect alone, then share the reflections in a dyad or triad with that subgroup coming to consensus on their position. Then dyads can be combined into quads with further clarification and consensus on issues. Groups can continue to combine with other groups until one or two larger groups have been able to find their common ground…and thus the common ground for the team.

Facilitation Skills

It is critical that all team members have the opportunity to gain facilitation skills including reflective listening, clarifying, open questioning, summarizing, encouraging, and reporting. Many teams prefer to rotate the role of the facilitator among members; other teams agree on a single facilitator for a specific period of time. Other important team roles include chairperson, process observer, recorder/reporter, critical friend, engaged participant, and, when required, translator. Garmston (2002) emphasizes that having all participants understand and agree to meeting roles is one of his five standards for successful meetings; the other four, all relevant for this **Group Process Guide**, are as follows:

- Address only one topic at a time.

- Use only one process (strategy) at a time.

- Achieve interactive and balanced participation.

- Use cognitive conflict productively.

The above commentary is a summary of the basic skills of facilitation. Later in the **Group Process Guide**, there is a more comprehensive discussion about facilitation skills in the context of team meetings (see School Improvement Meetings).

Go Round

Research has shown that those who speak aloud in the early part of any meeting are more likely to continue to speak and share throughout the meeting. The guidelines for a Go Round are that each person in the group responds to the prompt, in turn, without interruption or comment from the other members. Go Rounds are encouraged at the beginning of each session to bring all members into the group. Go Rounds can also be used at any time to get a sense of what each member of the group is thinking—or when one or two members tend to dominate the discussion, to ensure that all ideas have the opportunity to be shared. Go Rounds are an excellent strategy for mobilizing the interactive and balanced participation recommended by Garmston (2002).

Team Listing

For some group activities, it is important to have one team member record each participant's ideas, suggestions, and/or opinions on poster-sized paper. This Team Listing can be posted on the wall for easy reference and revision as needed.

Consensus Building

It is important to define consensus. Teams sometimes create problems (perhaps an intentional block to their success) by defining consensus as *everyone* in complete agreement on a course of action. While an admirable goal, this is rarely achieved. A more manageable definition of consensus is that of "sufficient consensus," defined as agreement among all members of the team that they will not sabotage the implementation of a course of action that is supported by the majority, even though there may be some skepticism regarding the likelihood of its success.

There are a variety of strategies that can be used to facilitate consensus and to determine if a majority opinion exists for a course of action. A Go Round with members stating their position on a scale of 1 (low support) to 10 (high support) can be very effective. Another technique is to have each member (on a count of three) give a signal, such as "thumbs up" for support; "thumb horizontal" for ambivalence; and "thumbs down" for non-support.

There are also many published strategies for creating a consensus opinion. These are available in many books on team building and group work. Examples include cooperative processing, nominal group technique, and brainstorming which will be discussed later in this workbook.

The Tambourine

This is an excellent group processing technique that can be used to enable a group of educators to meld their individual agendas and to find common ground. The technique is called the Tambourine because it resembles a tambourine when drawn on a large sheet of poster paper. The technique works as follows: the members of the group sit in a half circle around the sheet of paper—which can be pinned to a wall or affixed to a stand. It should look like the design below.

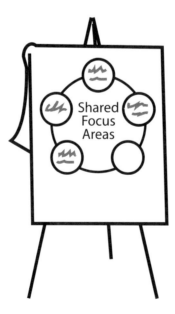

Then each individual, after careful consideration of the issues at hand, goes through his or her list of personal thoughts and ideas. The recorder/scribe writes these on the poster—within the small circle representing this particular member. This step is repeated for each individual until all the small circles are completed. Ten minutes are then devoted to silent scrutiny of what has been produced so far—with an eye to finding the "common ground" issues. Then, using a Go Round, members identify those items that are predominately in common and, if the majority of participants agree, the items are added to the inside of the larger circle—thus producing a shared agenda of common ground issues to which everyone has contributed.

Confronting Issues

Sometimes referred to as dealing with the "elephant in the living room," groups must be willing and able to identify those things that pose barriers to their effectiveness and to openly discuss the issues and seek mutually beneficial solutions. Confronting issues will often throw a team into chaos (the **Storming** phase) and can seem like a setback when a team has appeared to be functioning well. However, if the stages of group processing are thought of as a spiral, each time a group cycles through the phases they emerge at a higher level on the spiral than the last time around. Although difficult and challenging, it is the act of confronting barrier issues that increases the likelihood of long-term success of any team. The **GROUND RULES** again become critical in helping the group discuss their problems and find solutions.

Celebrations and Closure

On an ongoing basis, groups should engage in celebrations of their accomplishments and as closure at the conclusion of their work. These celebrations should be as public as possible and should recognize the contributions of all team members. The nature of each celebration is determined by the culture of the group—from solemn, ceremonial celebrations to more party-like atmospheres.

The quality of shared decision making based on data is dependent on the quality of collaborative processes used. This **Group Process Guide** is intended to give teams the tools they need to develop quality group-work sessions. Teams are also encouraged to use other sources of group processing strategies and to avail themselves of learning/training opportunities for facilitation skills if available.

The Next Layer of Teamwork Skills

In the first workbook in this series, *Conceptualizing a New Path*, the emphasis was on the acquisition and use of basic teamwork skills and techniques—including group processing, ground rules, the circle configuration, and Go Rounds—as discussed above. In fact, these skills are so foundational to the effective functioning of teams that they will reappear at various intervals throughout this second workbook. In what amounts to a "layered" approach, these basic skills now have to be combined with other kinds of skills and techniques that have a particular usefulness for teams and team members given responsibility for generating data-driven school improvement processes. These additional skills and techniques will be discussed in the following sections of the **Group Process Guide**.

Strategies for Establishing Priorities

There are numerous techniques that can be used for establishing priorities (in addition to the Tambourine discussed in the previous section) including the Diamond, the Prioritizing Grid, Onion Peeling, Pareto Analysis, Cooperative Processing, Fist of Five, and Weighted Voting. Each of these techniques is described and illustrated in this section. They should be reviewed in Chapter 2—Stage 3: Establishing Priorities for Improvement when teams are asked to prioritize school improvement issues.

The Diamond

This technique helps you select the top three items from a list of nine. Each of the nine major issues is written on a card (or self-adhesive sheet) and, in small teams, the cards are placed in ascending order with the most important issues at the top of the diamond. The small teams then report out and consensus is reached across the entire group.

The Prioritizing Grid

In a manner similar to the "Diamond," ten issues can be addressed and placed in priority order. The instructions on the following page explain the process.

The Prioritizing Grid

Here is a method for taking ten items and deciding which one is most important to you, which is next important, and so on.

First, list (up to) ten items, or choices, or needs....They do not need to be in order of importance.

1. _____   6. _____

2. _____   7. _____

3. _____   8. _____

4. _____   9. _____

5. _____   10. _____

Now compare the items you listed with each of the others using this grid. Circle the preferred one in each pair in rows **A** through **I**.

A	1 2							
B	1 3	2 3						
C	1 4	2 4	3 4					
D	1 5	2 5	3 5	4 5				
E	1 6	2 6	3 6	4 6	5 6			
F	1 7	2 7	3 7	4 7	5 7	6 7		
G	1 8	2 8	3 8	4 8	5 8	6 8	7 8	
H	1 9	2 9	3 9	4 9	5 9	6 9	7 9	8 9
I	1 10	2 10	3 10	4 10	5 10	6 10	7 10	8 10	9 10

Total the times each number was circled. Enter these totals in the spaces below.

1. ____ 2. ____ 3. ____ 4. ____ 5. ____ 6. ____ 7. ____ 8. ____ 9. ____ 10. ____

Relist the items in the order of priority to you (i.e., the item circled most often is first, and so on).

1. _____   6. _____

2. _____   7. _____

3. _____   8. _____

4. _____   9. _____

5. _____   10. _____

Onion Peeling

This is an excellent technique for organizing your data analysis and for deepening your understanding. The first step is to arrange the emerging themes or issues in the outer boxes of the top circle. The second step is to select the highest priority among them and place it in the inner circle. The next step is to place the same priority in the inner circle below and then brainstorm the reasons why this particular issue was selected as the priority. Each of the reasons is inserted in one of the outer boxes in the bottom circle. The last two steps can be repeated for any of the issues identified above.

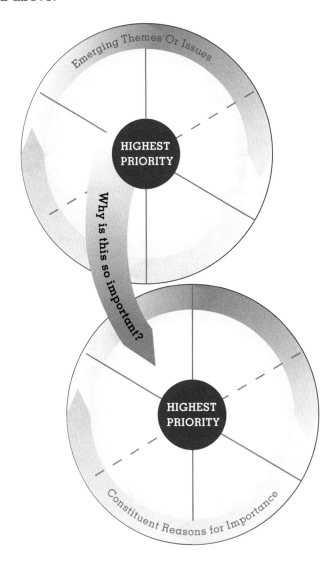

Pareto Analysis

Somewhat similar to "onion-peeling," this technique can be used to deepen your understanding by breaking down the priority area into its constituent parts. The instructions are found on the following page.

AN EXAMPLE OF PARETO ANALYSIS

In what academic areas are our students struggling the most?

READING

FOCUS HERE

WRITING

MATH

SCIENCE

LEADS TO

With what items/objectives are these students struggling the most?

COMPREHENSION

FOCUS HERE

VOCABULARY

DECODING

LEADS TO

What skills do our students need to focus on to improve?

DRAWING CONCLUSIONS

FOCUS GRADE-LEVEL **SMART** GOAL HERE

FINDING MAIN ORDER

WORDS IN CONTEXT

FACTS AND DETAILS

By targeting the most problematic academic area and progressively breaking it into smaller elements, teachers can focus instruction where the most significant academic gains can occur.
EDUCATIONAL LEADERSHIP/FEBRUARY 2000

Cooperative Processing

This is a much lengthier, more sophisticated process. It involves several "rounds" of both individual and group work. Again, a detailed description of the various steps that compose the overall process is provided below.

Assign two roles: facilitator and recorder

Facilitator:

- Initiates session

- Monitors process

- Provides opportunity for everyone to speak

- Monitors that everyone speaks in turn

- Monitors so that one person speaks at a time

Recorder:

- Records statements

- Does not edit

- Numbers each item

Step One: In-Turn Response/Individual Contributions

Step Two: In-Turn Response/Clarification

Step Three: In-Turn Response/Discussion (Pros/Cons)

Step Four: Decision/Voting Component
        (Clear-out Voting; Weighted Voting)

Individual Reflection/In-Turn Response

- Each individual reflects on the question.

- Individuals write responses using single words or short phrases, if possible.

- No talking.

- In-turn response: each person states one response at a time only or says, "pass."

- Each member has the opportunity to pass and yet reenter whenever he/she wishes.

- There is no mention of any item already recorded.

- There is no discussion or clarification allowed during In-Turn Response time.

Elements of In-Turn Response

- Everyone is given an equal opportunity to participate.

- Everyone's contribution is accepted.

- "Pass" rule forces everyone to participate.

- If the process continues until each person passes in consecutive order, no one can say he/she did not have an opportunity to speak.

- This is an efficient means of gathering information or soliciting opinions when no decisions need to be made.

Clarification Component

- Examine items for clear understanding.

- Explanation is given by the person who contributed the item.

- Clarify only. No discussion!

- Use in-turn response and "pass" rule.

Discussion Component
(Pro/Con Statements)

PRO

- Speak on behalf of any item on the list.

- No debate!

- Do not repeat opinions already stated.

CON

- Speak on behalf of eliminating an item.

- No debate!

- Do not repeat opinions already stated.

Decision/Voting Component
(Clear-Out Voting)

- Use majority rule.

- Consider each item.

- Vote opened hand for YES, closed hand for NO.

- Everyone must vote on each item. YOU CANNOT PASS!

- If the majority votes "no" on an item, it is removed from the list.

Decision/Voting Component
(Weighted Voting)

- Vote by assigning a value to each item.

- Highest rating is group selection.

- Conduct final vote by YES/NO, if necessary.

- Vote on each item. YOU CANNOT PASS!

Reasons for using Cooperative Processing: Equal opportunities for contributing ideas:

- forces participation

- prevents domination

- focuses the group at all times

- encourages a higher degree of efficiency

- promotes better communication

Resource: Cooperative Processing by Norman Public Schools. Norman, Oklahoma and I-LEAD (1991)

"Fist of Five" and "Weighted Voting" Consensus Building

These are two simpler consensus techniques that may be used independently or during some of the processes listed above.

Fist of Five	Weighted Voting
5 = Total Agreement	3 = Highest importance
4 = Yes. High on my list.	2 = Very important
3 = It's an OK idea. I can go along with it.	1 = Somewhat important
2 = Don't agree. Won't support, but won't sabotage.	If you have:
1 = Bad idea. Will sabotage.	• 0-20 options; each person may be allocated 3-3's, 3-2's, & 3-1's
Fist= = Worst idea I've ever heard. Will sabotage.	• 21-24 options; 4 of each weighting (3,2,1)
	• 35 & above: 5 of each weighting (3,2,1)
	• Can't place more than 1/3 of your total votes on any one option.
	• All assigned votes must be used.
	All votes must be cast as whole numbers.

Techniques for Generating Ideas and Information Sharing

During the ongoing process of school improvement, there is a recurring need for team members to generate ideas and share information. Several techniques for generating ideas and information sharing—which are all utilized in this workbook—are introduced below. More sophisticated and lengthier processes like Cooperative Processing and the Nominal Group Technique (NGT)—which involve a combination of skills and techniques—are included as major activities in the main body of this workbook.

Brainstorming

According to *Pocket Tools for Education* (1996), brainstorming is the free, uninhibited generation of ideas, usually in a group setting, and is used to solicit ideas from the group members on a given topic. In terms of running a brainstorming session, it is important to follow these four steps: select a recorder and group facilitator, generate ideas, record the ideas, and organize the results.

The goals of brainstorming as described in the same publication are to

- generate a wide variety and extensive number of ideas

- ensure that everyone on the team becomes involved in the problem-solving process

- ensure that nothing is overlooked

- create an atmosphere of creativity and openness

In addition, the group facilitator should maintain the following rules:

- No criticism is allowed.

- Everyone has an equal opportunity to express ideas.

- Quantity is emphasized over quality.

- Piggybacking or hitchhiking (adding to, elaborating or supporting someone else's idea) is encouraged.

Variations on the brainstorming theme are explained on the following pages.

Free-Wheel Brainstorm

Individuals are encouraged to spontaneously call out responses, remembering to abide by the following guidelines:

- **B**uild on each other's ideas.

- **R**efrain from judgment.

- **A**im for quantity.

- **I**magine creatively and out of the box.

- **N**ote all suggestions.

Round-Robin Brainstorm

Each participant takes a turn in giving an idea or suggestion. An individual may "pass" at any time and may re-enter the process to give a response—again, at any time. Continue going from person to person in the group until everyone passes. Once again, the B.R.A.I.N. guidelines should be applied.

Round Robin

The round-robin approach can be used for purposes other than brainstorming and generating ideas (e.g., expressing personal opinions or sharing information). It is important to follow the agreed upon rules and, in so doing, protect each speaker and his/her contribution.

Directions for conducting a Round Robin: Designate a person to start (e.g., the person to the left of the facilitator or the person with a birthday nearest to the current date). Go around in a circle, giving each person a turn to share his/her opinions or information concerning the topic in question. There should be no response from anyone else, with the exception that the group member recording each contribution may ask questions for clarification.

The facilitator should model for all participants a non-judgmental attitude in listening. Attention should be focused on the speaker and what he/she has to say, with the facilitator remembering to avoid making negative or positive responses to the statements. The reason for this strict adherence to limited responses is that other participants might hear the response as limiting their contribution (thinking that what they've got to say will either be treated just as negatively or not viewed in such a positive light).

Round Table

The same procedure as for a Round Robin is followed with the exception that the opinions/ideas are first written on index cards or self-adhering notes and then shared.

Turn to Your Partner

Formulate: Think of your own answer individually.

Share: Share thoughts with one other person.

Listen: Listen carefully to another person's ideas/explanations.

Combine: Build on each other's thoughts and ideas.

Team Discussion

Talk it over; share your ideas. The important focus of the team discussion is that the team has a goal in mind; a specific outcome from the discussion such as, "What do we believe will be the best measure of success of our students' mastery of reading comprehension?"

Three-Step Interview

Group of 4-6 divided into pairs (dyads)

Interview: Set time limit per partner interview and round robin (usually 3-5 minutes per interview and 8-10 minutes for sharing).

Step One: Partner 1 interviews Partner 2
Partner 3 interviews Partner 4

Step Two: Reverse roles

Step Three: Each person shares the partner's response with the whole group (round robin) or with another dyad.

Techniques for Processing Data-Driven School Improvement

There is another category of skills and techniques that is pertinent to the process of school improvement itself. Techniques for using the ideas generated, problem solving, planning, decision making, and prioritizing fall into this category, as do all the skills necessary for the collection, analysis, and reporting of data. Indeed, throughout this workbook, various techniques and activities are included that, when applied in planning and decision-making sessions, activate the stages of data-driven school improvement. These stages, taken together, constitute the process framework known as the CREATE model for school improvement that was first introduced in Workbook One and which provides the structure for Chapter Two of this workbook. Again, the six stages are:

- Constructing a Shared Vision

- Reviewing Current Practice

- Establishing Priorities

- Action Planning

- Taking the Action

- Evaluating Progress

This workbook contains many techniques and activities that can be used by school-based teams at each of these stages of the cyclical process of school improvement. By applying the techniques in their local contexts, users of this workbook will be *doing* school improvement. Indeed, what is significant about this workbook is its practicality and relevance. It is more a handbook than a training manual. By undertaking the tasks and activities, team members will be working on data-driven and continuous school improvement and making it happen.

SCHOOL IMPROVEMENT MEETINGS

Structuring Learning Team Meetings

Before the meeting…

Adequate preparation before each team meeting by both the facilitator and team members will result in more productive team meetings. Based on the length of each team meeting, the facilitator must decide what material will be covered in the meeting and what material participants will need to cover on their own in preparation for the meeting. For example, in preparing for the first meeting to begin discussing Chapter One of Workbook Two, the facilitator might ask team members to read on their own, prior to meeting, the sections explaining the first pre-condition for effective school improvement planning.

The facilitator must also decide which tasks/activities will be implemented in any given meeting. Each task in the workbook is organized as follows:

<u>Purpose:</u> (Why are we doing this task?)

<u>Grouping:</u> (How are we to work—on our own, in pairs or triads, or with the whole Learning Team?)

<u>Group process strategy:</u> (Which strategy will most effectively support us in accomplishing the work we are doing?)

<u>Directions:</u> (What are we doing?)

It is important for the facilitator to carefully study these four elements of a task prior to the meeting to ensure a smooth implementation of the task. Each group process strategy is explained in the **Group Process Guide**, which will serve as a handy reference throughout the use of the workbook. In addition, it is the facilitator's responsibility to ensure that any necessary materials, such as poster paper and markers, are ready for use.

During the meeting…

The group processing skills that have just been covered in the **Group Process Guide** are most frequently used in meetings. Indeed, it is in meetings that school improvement work is generally processed. For the benefit of all those concerned, such meetings need to be focused, purposeful, task-oriented, and productive. There is nothing that gives school improvement a bad name more than meetings that meander aimlessly into educators' personal time. Meetings—and the time used for meetings—are resources that we cannot afford to squander. At any school improvement meeting, therefore, the basic skills and techniques learned and applied in the first workbook, *Conceptualizing a New Path*, need to be practiced in combination to provide for structure, flow, and, above all, task completion. In each meeting, these simple procedural rules should be utilized:

- Assign team member roles.
- Review the ground rules.

- Conduct a focus activity or "ice-breaker."

- Review the goal(s) of the meeting and check for understanding.

- Select an appropriate process to match and accomplish the task.

- Record the conversation by displaying the key words and phrases used.

- Provide time to reflect at the end of the meeting.

Indeed, this checklist is a very handy tool for group facilitators to use when planning school improvement meetings. Moreover, during the reflection time at the end of the meeting, it may well be advisable to invite team members to evaluate the session using the kind of review sheet below.

Team Self-Review Sheet

For each of the following statements, circle the number which best indicates your view of how your group performed, using the continuum of "1" (Strongly Disagree) to "10" (Strongly Agree).

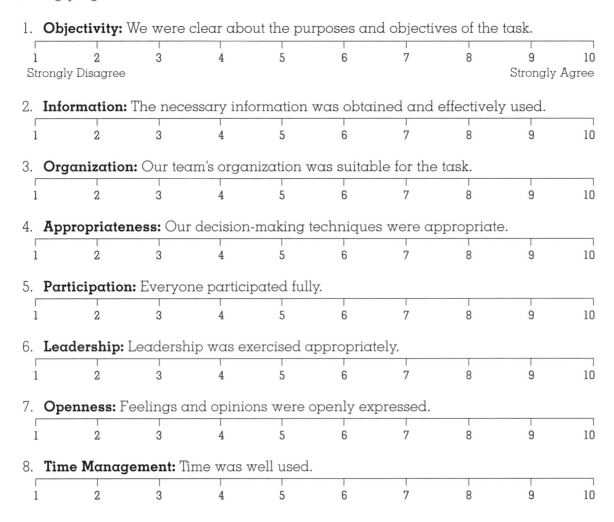

1. **Objectivity:** We were clear about the purposes and objectives of the task.

| 1 | 2 | 3 | 4 | 5 | 6 | 7 | 8 | 9 | 10 |
Strongly Disagree   Strongly Agree

2. **Information:** The necessary information was obtained and effectively used.

| 1 | 2 | 3 | 4 | 5 | 6 | 7 | 8 | 9 | 10 |

3. **Organization:** Our team's organization was suitable for the task.

| 1 | 2 | 3 | 4 | 5 | 6 | 7 | 8 | 9 | 10 |

4. **Appropriateness:** Our decision-making techniques were appropriate.

| 1 | 2 | 3 | 4 | 5 | 6 | 7 | 8 | 9 | 10 |

5. **Participation:** Everyone participated fully.

| 1 | 2 | 3 | 4 | 5 | 6 | 7 | 8 | 9 | 10 |

6. **Leadership:** Leadership was exercised appropriately.

| 1 | 2 | 3 | 4 | 5 | 6 | 7 | 8 | 9 | 10 |

7. **Openness:** Feelings and opinions were openly expressed.

| 1 | 2 | 3 | 4 | 5 | 6 | 7 | 8 | 9 | 10 |

8. **Time Management:** Time was well used.

| 1 | 2 | 3 | 4 | 5 | 6 | 7 | 8 | 9 | 10 |

9. **Collaboration:** I enjoyed working in the group.

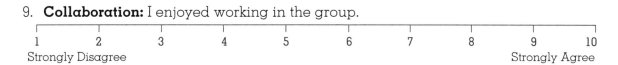

1	2	3	4	5	6	7	8	9	10

Strongly Disagree   Strongly Agree

10. What might the team do differently to improve the next meeting?

A Closer Examination of Facilitation Skills

Given the task orientation of the teamwork, the countless meetings that underpin the school improvement process, and the concomitant need for productivity, the success of school improvement teams cannot be left to chance. While Weisbord and Janoff (1995) maintain that the members of "self-managed groups"—that come together during one-time brainstorming workshops or planning sessions—can organize their own work without a facilitator at their table, in the kind of ongoing teamwork envisioned in this series of workbooks, the role of the facilitator (whether rotated or not) and the application of facilitation skills are seen as absolutely vital. Indeed, in their path-finding work on group processing (*The Adaptive School*, 1999) Garmston and Wellman have emphasized the crucial importance of the facilitator's role. In terms that go to the heart of this workbook series, they identify the core values that should guide the process of facilitation:

■ **Valid information**

People share all information relevant to an issue, using specific examples so that others can determine independently if the information is true. People understand the information given to them.

■ **Free and informed choice**

People can define their own objectives and the methods for achieving them and that their choices are based on valid information.

■ **Internal commitment to the choice**

People feel personally responsible for the choices they make.

Moreover, argue Garmston and Wellman (1999), facilitators should be able to call on a knowledge base that includes understanding of Self, Groups, Strategies and Moves, and Maps (see next page).

Knowledge Base for Facilitators

MAPS

Facilitators seek to understand meetings and make decisions affecting meeting dynamics with the aid of four types of mental models:

1. Universal meeting goals

2. Structures for meeting success

3. Energy management

4. Principles of effective meeting transactions, information processing, and interventions

SELF

Facilitators' most sensitive and critical asset is themselves. Self-knowledge of cognitive style, educational beliefs, emotional states, intentions, strengths, and limitations permits facilitation decisions to be based on group needs rather than personal preferences.

STRATEGIES AND MOVES

Facilitators manage and direct meeting processes. They know and use a range of facilitation strategies and moves to manage group: energy, information, and action.

GROUPS

Although all groups have common tendencies, each group has unique characteristics that facilitators must take into account: culture, developmental level, group dynamics and history, relationship with facilitator, external environment, and conflicting demands.

Garmston and Wellman (1999)

According to Garmston and Wellman, the facilitator's knowledge of "Self" includes a self-examination using such questions as

- Who am I? What do I care about? How much do I dare?

- Who is my client? For whom am I working?

- What are my desired outcomes in this setting?

- How is my expertise simultaneously an asset and a liability?

- How can I distinguish between right and being effective?

- What lenses do I wear?

- What types of capacities do I need to develop for this assignment?

This list of questions includes a timely warning to any facilitator—there may be things that he/she says or does that potentially impede rather than enhance the group process.

In terms of knowledge about "Strategies and Moves," Garmston and Wellman (1999) argue that the facilitator should understand how to "Manage Energy," "Manage Information," and "Manage Actions." These distinctions are crucial for an understanding of how teams (and their facilitators) should go about processing school improvement issues. "Managing Energy" involves getting the team members mobilized to work together. "Managing Information" is concerned with the generation and organization of ideas. "Managing Actions" entails deciding what to do with the ideas. In addition, the same authors provide a most useful self-assessment instrument for a facilitator to use when reflecting on his/her role performance, as shown below.

PAYING ATTENTION TO THE FACILITATION PROCESS	
	Notes and Reflections
Clarifies the purpose	
Creates ownership for the proposed challenge	
Checks assumptions	
Clarifies and reinforces norms	
Establishes the process	
Sets time frames	
Stays neutral and objective	
Paraphrases appropriately	
Acts lively and positively	
Makes clear notes	
Asks effective probing questions	
Makes helpful process suggestions	
Encourages participation	
Addresses conflict	
Sets an effective pace	
Checks the process	
Transitions smoothly to new topics	
Makes clear and timely summaries	
Knows when to stop	

Garmston and Wellman (1999)

School Improvement Meetings
Task 1: Assessing Current Facilitation Efforts

Purpose: To assess the effectiveness of the facilitation of school improvement meetings in the participants' schools and districts.

Grouping: Work with your Learning Team.

Directions: Using the same assessment instrument as described above, in your teams, discuss the effectiveness of current facilitation efforts in your local school improvement meetings. Which items could be considered strengths and which are definitely challenges for those concerned?

A Word About Teams

This workbook can be used on two levels: in off-site school improvement training sessions where the participants may or may not be from the same school or school district or during on-site school improvement planning sessions where the teams will be the site-based teams mentioned in the introduction. Whichever is the case, participants will get the most out of this workbook when they are members of a locally based team and are using the various tasks "for real" (i.e., they are using this workbook to actually do school improvement).

Participants—whether working directly in their schools or returning to their schools following the training sessions—may well want to work within the protection of the kind of Operational Agreement recommended in the first workbook in this series. An example is as follows:

This school encourages students, parents, staff, and community members to put forth a sincere effort to interact in the following ways:

- Have the best interests of our students as a central focus at all times.

- Be flexible and receptive to others' ideas through

    - actively listening to each other

    - honest and open exchange of ideas

    - sensitivity in the use of humor

    - acceptance of disagreements as a necessary part of the decision-making process

- Work toward inclusiveness by encouraging and welcoming the involvement of all.

- Respect the integrity of decisions made by other individuals and groups.

Establishing such a school-wide Operational Agreement is a high priority task for any teams embarking on the journey of school improvement.

Notes

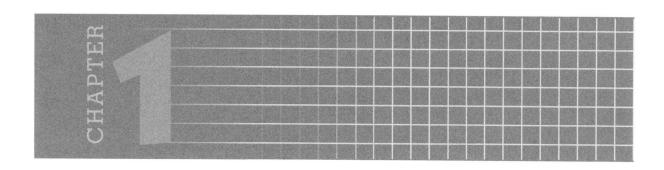

CHAPTER ONE: PRE-CONDITIONS FOR EFFECTIVE SCHOOL IMPROVEMENT PLANNING

While the first workbook in this series, *Conceptualizing a New Path*, provided an overview of data-based decision making and its role in the educational change process, this second workbook focuses on data-driven school improvement in schools, and, specifically, the role of data-based decision making within the process of school improvement planning and implementation.

In order to fully benefit from the guidance contained in this workbook, it is vital that schools and school districts attend to four pre-conditions:

- a willingness to commit to building and maintaining high performance teams for processing local school improvement efforts

- a willingness to commit to integrated planning

- a willingness to commit to school improvement efforts that are data-driven

- a willingness to commit to using a process framework for school improvement planning and implementation

As an introduction to this workbook, each of these pre-conditions will be examined in turn.

Pre-Condition 1: A Willingness to Commit to Building and Maintaining High Performance Teams for Processing Local School Improvement Efforts

Working in teams is an essential element of working on data-driven school improvement efforts. Consequently, for school improvement efforts to be successful, working *effectively* in high performance teams is a crucial requirement.

Conducting data-driven school improvement activities requires different kinds of teams, as follows:

- **School Improvement Team** (SIT) is a standing committee and acts as the steering group for the entire school improvement process. It should be composed of representatives from all stakeholder groups and should meet on a very regular (e.g., bi-weekly) basis.

- **Study Groups** can play a vital role within the data-driven school improvement process. They can be used for studying both internal and external data and for identifying potential interventions and strategies to recommend to colleagues. Their job is to investigate what options are available to meet the identified needs.

■ **Action Teams** represent goal areas within the school improvement process and are best used for action planning and leading colleagues into the early stages of implementation.

■ **Action Research Teams** (the subject of the third workbook in this series, *Engaging in Action Research*) are crucial during the long-term application, monitoring, and evaluation of implementation efforts.

Mapping the Team Structure for School Improvement

It is useful to show how these various teams connect. An example of such a school improvement flow chart (from Westwood Elementary School in Ankeny, Iowa) is included below.

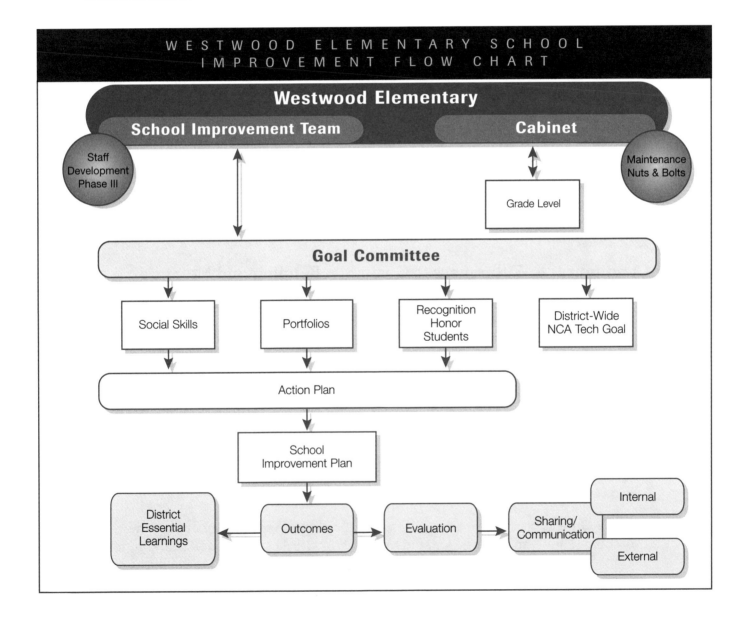

WESTWOOD ELEMENTARY SCHOOL IMPROVEMENT FLOW CHART

 Pre-Conditions ■ Task 1: Mapping the Connections
Between Local School Improvement Teams

<u>Purpose:</u> To understand how local school improvement efforts are currently structured by mapping the connections between the various teams involved.

<u>Grouping:</u> Work with your Learning Team.

<u>Directions:</u> In your school/district team, map the infrastructure for local school improvement efforts, making sure to include all the connections between the various site-based teams. Use the example above as a guide.

Unlike the School Improvement Team, Study Groups, Action Teams, and Action Research Teams have a more limited life span. They exist to fulfill a designated set of tasks during a particular stage (or stages) of the school improvement process. When these tasks are accomplished, their work is done. Having said that, however, their work may still take over a year (or more) to complete. From research on these more temporary kinds of teams, we know that they need to

- have a shared focus and a clearly stated mission/goal

- have a comparatively short life span

- be voluntary and formed on an "interest" basis

- be self-monitoring

- be linked to the organization's mainstream decision-making process

- have clearly defined targets

- have targets that are achievable

- meet on the "firm's" time

- have their proposals given very serious consideration

Relative to Study Groups in particular, Carlene Murphy (1995) has made the following recommendations:

Membership

- six team members or less

- grade level or cross-grade/cross-representational

Meeting Schedule

- meet regularly (e.g., once a week for one hour)

- provide scheduled time within the school day

- release teachers for joint planning by creatively using "specials" in elementary schools and schedule planning time in middle and high schools

Group Process

- no special group training necessary

- informal leadership provides for non-hierarchical but task-oriented sessions

- log used to record team dialogue, ideas, and recommendations

- each group should decide its own particular focus, while the content of study is a decision made by the entire faculty

While Murphy provides several useful ideas, she tends to overplay the degree of informality required and downplay the developmental work that has to be done for teams to be successful. For teams charged with school improvement tasks to be successful, four skill sets are required. These form the content of the **Group Process Guide** for this workbook: basic teamwork skills, facilitation skills, techniques for generating ideas and information sharing, and techniques for processing data-driven school improvement.

Pre-Condition 2: A Willingness to Commit to Integrated Planning

The question of oneness is vital. Several years ago, the author walked into a small elementary school in England and, because it was his first visit, he asked to see their school improvement plan. "Which one would you like to see?" he was asked. "We have nine."

As he has said elsewhere, having nine school improvement plans in a school that size (or, for that matter, a school of any size) is the road to lunacy. Yet it is so easy to get into the same situation. The educators in the school in question wanted to do the right thing. They were very earnest in their belief that every time they received grant monies or were in receipt of the equivalent of state mandates and were asked to submit an improvement plan, this meant having to produce a new, separate plan. As the author said at the time—and has said in countless schools since then, "You only need one plan; just keep changing the introduction every time someone wants to give you money!"

This statement is not as subversive as it sounds. If goal accomplishment is the objective, then it is in everyone's interest that a school faculty becomes "packaged for success" (Holly, 1990)—by having one solid, data-based, achievable school improvement plan that, when implemented, will significantly impact student learning.

Guskey (1990) has argued cogently for the integration of change programs within improvement initiatives and the author (1989 and 1990) has emphasized that school improvement planning can be the vehicle for this integrative process. Indeed, school improvement plans are best seen not as part of the problem (of change overload) but as part of the solution (Holly, 1990).

Integrative planning processes should not only generate the fusion of change programs, but also, in the process, create opportunities for involving people—because we know that meaningful involvement leads to greater commitment to and ownership of the resulting school plan. Sparks (1994) and Murphy (1995) have both described the benefits of staff involvement in the process of school improvement planning—as a form of staff development. For his part, Sparks notes that staff development activities have been influenced by three main ideas:

- **results-driven education**, which acknowledges that virtually all students can acquire the school's valued outcomes provided they are given adequate time and appropriate instruction

- **systems thinking**, which emphasizes that, by working together, a school staff cannot only reap the benefits of synergism (where the whole is greater than the sum of the parts) but also can identify those high leverage growth points (see Senge, 1990) that can have a significant impact on the organization

- **constructivism**, which entails self-learning and the building of a change agenda through collaboration with peers and outside support but in one's own context

School improvement planning has been heavily influenced by these same three ideas. It is now almost axiomatic that planning efforts in schools are directed at improving student learning results, involve the orchestration of collective staff endeavor, and are predicated on the notions of self-development and self-renewal. Indeed, according to Sparks (1994):

> School improvement too often has been based on fad rather than on a clear, compelling vision of the school system's future. This, in turn, has led to one-shot staff development workshops with no thought given to follow-up, nor to how this technique fits in with those that were taught in previous years. At its worst, teachers are asked to implement poorly understood innovations with little support and assistance, and before they are able to approach mastery, the school has moved on to another area.

> An orientation to outcomes and systems thinking has led to strategic planning at the district, school, and departmental levels. Clear, compelling mission statements and measurable objectives expressed in terms of student outcomes give guidance to the type of staff development activities that would best serve district and school goals....This comprehensive approach to change makes certain that all aspects of the system are working in tandem toward a manageable set of outcomes that are valued throughout the system.

> More attention today is being directed at helping schools meet their improvement goals. Schools set their goals both to assist the school system in

achieving its long-term objectives and to address challenges unique to their students' needs.

School improvement efforts in which the entire staff seeks incremental annual improvement related to a set of common objectives (e.g., helping all students become better problem solvers, increasing the number of students who participate in a voluntary community service program to 100%) over a three to five year span are viewed as the key to significant reform.

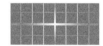 ## Pre-Conditions
Task 2: Rating Current Performance

Purpose: To return to some of the themes of the first workbook, *Conceptualizing a New Path*, and invite participants to rate their school's current performance in terms of generating staff development efforts that are working in the service of school improvement.

Grouping: Work with your Learning Team.

Directions: The following statements are based on some of the themes in the Spark's passage. Work as a team to rate your school's efforts for each statement using a 1 to 5 scale with 1 being "Poor" to 5 being "Outstanding."

Change faddism is being replaced by the pursuit of a clear, compelling vision.

| 1 | 2 | 3 | 4 | 5 |

Idiosyncratic, fragmented activities are giving way to staff working in tandem toward a valued and manageable set of learning outcomes.

| 1 | 2 | 3 | 4 | 5 |

Teacher interest-based goals are changing to goals that are based on the unique learning needs of students.

| 1 | 2 | 3 | 4 | 5 |

Piecemeal innovation is being replaced by incremental growth.

| 1 | 2 | 3 | 4 | 5 |

Guskey (1990) explores these same issues. His main point is that proponents of new programmatic ideas promote their favorites without seeing connections to other strategies. It's up to school leaders, he says, to discover how to integrate a collection of programs and strategies within their improvement initiatives. In addition, he makes the following points:

- All of the innovative strategies in the improvement program should share common goals and premises.

- There is no single innovative strategy that can do everything; no single strategy can solve the diversity of problems that schools typically face. Indeed, he emphasizes, it is only when several strategies are carefully and systematically integrated that sustained improvement in learning becomes possible.

- Innovative strategies in the improvement program should complement each other and presenters (who are normally blind to the advantages of any strategies but their own) should explain to educators how they connect. Hatch (2002) has recently made much the same point.

- Citing the research of Berman (1976), Guskey maintains that all innovative strategies need to be adapted to suit the conditions of individual classrooms and buildings.

- Agreeing with Fullan (1982) and Joyce and Showers (1982), Guskey argues for supporting innovating teachers well beyond the first year of implementation.

- When a well-conceived combination of innovative strategies is used, the results are likely to be greater than those attained using any single strategy. Guskey attributes this to the "additive" effect of implementing complementary strategies in concert.

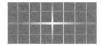 Pre-Conditions ▪ Task 3: Integrating Programs and Strategies in Local Contexts

Purpose: To prompt participant reflection on the extent to which Guskey's advice has been heeded and acted upon in their local contexts.

Grouping: Work with your Learning Team.

<u>Group process strategy:</u> Use the Round-Robin Brainstorming technique. Select a team recorder and create a Team List.

<u>Directions:</u> Working as a team, think about your own situation and brainstorm as many indications as you can that your local school system has heeded some or all of Guskey's messages. The Round Robin Brainstorm technique described in the **Group Process Guide** would be most appropriate to use with this task. The team recorder will record all responses on a Team List.

Unlike Sparks, Guskey (1990) does not recommend using an incremental approach, presumably because, to him, it represents a version of the "single strategy" approach and not the combined, concerted approach that he is advocating. The question arises, however, whether "incrementalism" can be used to produce the same kind of combined, additive effect that Guskey is promoting—but over time and not simultaneously. Perhaps this story (taken from a BBC radio broadcast) will help our thinking.

The Sony Walkman® Story

The Walkman has been a huge success story—like most of Sony's inventions. Apparently, this does not happen by accident. The employees of Sony work incredibly hard to make their products successful. With the Walkman, however, especially in the early, pre-production days, things did not go smoothly. Various prototypes came and went—without ever being marketed. They didn't survive the rigorous field-testing used by Sony and broke down too easily and too regularly for mass public consumption. Eventually, however, one particular design proved much more reliable—reliable enough for the marketing department to plan a public launch. The rest is history—but not quite. Some fifteen years on, the basic product—on the inside—is still very much the same as the first machine to arrive in the stores. The packaging has changed many times, as has the number of models available. There's a Sports Walkman, a Jogger's Walkman, a child's model, an in-car version, etc. Over the years the machine itself has been updated, but never changed dramatically. The Walkman is a classic story of adding to, and recycling, a winning design.

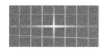 Pre-Conditions
Task 4: Relating the Sony Story to Education

<u>Purpose:</u> To reflect on the significance of the Sony Walkman story and its relevance for how we should go about change in education.

<u>Grouping:</u> Work in small groups of four people.

<u>Group process strategy:</u> Use the Three-Step Interview (refer to the **Group Process Guide**).

<u>Directions:</u> In answering the following questions, form into small groups (of four members) and apply the technique known as the Three-Step Interview.

What is significant about this story? What is there about the story that we could apply to great effect in education? What are some examples of how this could most effectively be done in education?

Carlene Murphy sees study groups as part of the solution to the problem of not integrating change initiatives. Study groups, she says, can help integrate and bring coherence to a school's collection of instructional strategies, models, and programs. In words very reminiscent of those used in the first workbook of this series, she points out that schools are continually bombarded with innovations. Indeed, she recounts an experience very similar to the "bubble map" story from the first workbook, *Conceptualizing a New Path*.

When she asked a group of teachers to list all of the innovations that had been introduced over the previous five years and to indicate whether they were at the initiation stage, the implementation stage, or the institutionalization stage of the change process, they responded by placing 18 changes at the initiation stage and 22 at implementation. Significantly, none of the changes were placed at the institutionalization stage. Given the continuing bombardment and the ensuing lack of "embedded-ness" and continuation, Murphy argues that study groups can sift through the changes (both potential and actual), noting their similarities and differences and identifying how the similarities can be used to cluster and synthesize the changes into integrated packages—as recommended by Guskey (1990).

Pre-Conditions
Task 5: Listing Local Change Initiatives

<u>Purpose:</u> To personalize and localize the discussion by inviting participants to list the change initiatives with which they've been involved over the last five years and to classify them in terms of the degree of "embedded-ness" attained.

<u>Grouping:</u> Work with your Learning Team.

<u>Group process strategy:</u> Use the Free-Wheel Brainstorm technique (refer to the **Group Process Guide**).

<u>Directions:</u> It is now your opportunity to undertake the task suggested by Carlene Murphy. In the chart on the next page, and working as a school team, brainstorm a list (using the Free-Wheel Brainstorm technique) of all the changes that have been introduced in your school over the last five years. Next to each change, indicate whether it has reached the initiation stage, the implementation stage, or the institutional stage of the change process.

List of Changes	Initiation	Implementation	Institutional

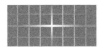

Pre-Conditions
Task 6: Creating Integrated Change Packages

Purpose: To act on the advice given by Murphy and Guskey and create integrated change packages.

Grouping: Work with your Learning Team.

Directions: Again, working as a school team, look at all the changes that you have listed in Task 5 and discuss how your school could gain from the more integrated approach described by Carlene Murphy and Thomas Guskey. As a result of your discussion, list here the change packages that could be constructed to help your change efforts become more integrated, more synthesized, and, probably, more institutionalized by sifting through the changes (both potential and actual), noting their similarities and differences and identifying how the similarities can be used to cluster and synthesize the changes into integrated change packages.

Integrated change packages:

Pre-Condition 3: A Willingness to Commit to School Improvement Efforts That are Data-Driven

A second theme touched on by Carlene Murphy brings us to the central purpose of this workbook. Study groups, she says, can be used to inject data-based decision making into a school's improvement efforts. In fact, in study groups, two kinds of data can be collected and analyzed: external data and internal data (see Holly, 2003).

External Data

Collecting external data entails studying the external knowledge base (see Calhoun, 1999) and what Murphy refers to as research on teaching and learning—in order, she says, to make wiser, research-based decisions. In so doing, she argues, teachers become more objective about teaching and learning practices, less subjectively tied to their personally favorite strategies, and more ready to end their classroom isolation and join with other colleagues in learning how to implement some of the research-based strategies in their classrooms.

Internal Data

Collecting internal data enables staff members to learn about the current functioning of their school. In her work, Murphy encourages teachers to study at least six data sources from the following list:

- test results

- discipline referrals (how many and why)

- suspensions (how many and why)

- incidents and types of violent behavior

- distribution of student grades by reporting periods

- parental involvement in school functions

- community perceptions of the school

- responses to questionnaires by parents, teachers, and students

- promotion and retention rates

- amounts of independent reading by students (including circulation reports from the school library)

- staff use of resources

- reports from accrediting agencies

- staff resignations and transfers (how many and why)

These internal data can be used to identify priorities for improvement, while the fruits of the external data search—the research-based strategies—can be matched to these identified needs. Internal data reveal our problems; external data produce the solutions. What is crucial is that the "what" (the selected changes) match the "why" (the targeted needs). Indeed, Murphy points out that data-based decision making is the vehicle for helping staff to connect the "what" with the "why." They have to understand that this particular change has been selected because it has a known track record of meeting this particular identified need. Indeed, the large phalanx of teachers who, when it comes to change, tend to want to wait and see are the ones who have a need to know the "why" before they climb on board the "what" (in the first workbook, the "yes, buts" descriptor was used for this group of educators [see Hampel, 1995]).

It is vital that these people see something very different from the situation to which they are accustomed—one which has been described as "too many solutions chasing too few (identified) problems" (Holly, 1996). It is these somewhat skeptical educators who need to become the stalwarts for school improvement. It is also vital that as many staff members as possible are involved in the process of rendering school improvement needs-based and data-driven. The belief is that if they are actively involved in the use of data (both to identify needs and select the changes to meet them), they will be much more likely to commit to implementation and follow-through.

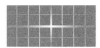

Pre-Conditions
Task 7: Identifying Internal Data Sources

Purpose: To begin to consider what internal data sources are regularly consulted in the participants' schools and school districts.

Grouping: Work with your Learning Team.

Group process strategy: Use the Round-Table Brainstorming and the Team List (refer to the Group Process Guide).

<u>Directions:</u> Working as a school team, create a list of the internal data sources that are regularly consulted in your school and/or school district (using the Round-Table procedure).

Internal Data Sources

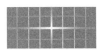 Pre-Conditions
Task 8: Identifying External Data Sources

Purpose: To begin to consider what external data sources are regularly consulted in the participants' schools and school districts.

Grouping: Work with your Learning Team.

Directions: In your team, answer these three questions:

1. What external data have been studied in your school/school district over the last five years?

2. What other needs were you attempting to meet?

3. What happened as a result of studying these external data?

Writing in 1990, Guskey made this observation:

> Administrators also vary in the criteria they use to select innovations for their improvement programs. Often they choose one set of strategies over another after careful consideration of pertinent evidence, such as results from a faculty needs survey, the scores from a comprehensive student testing program, or data gathered through a formal internal evaluation. More often, however, they select innovations on the basis of personal preferences or impressions. Sometimes the presentation style of the purveyor influences decision makers as much as the characteristics of the strategy itself.

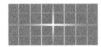 ## Pre-Conditions ■ Task 9: Gathering Evidence of Data-Driven Decision Making

<u>Purpose:</u> To explore to what extent interest-based decision making has been replaced by data-based decision making.

<u>Grouping:</u> Work individually and then with your Learning Team. Select a recorder/reporter.

<u>Directions:</u> Reflect individually on the above passage. Writing in the space below, provide evidence that, in your local school system, the first (needs-based data-driven) approach has gained preponderance over the second (interest-based) approach. Then, meet with your Learning Team to share and discuss your evidence. Appoint a recorder/reporter and ask that person to make notes during your discussion and then to share your team's evidence with the larger group (if applicable).

Pre-Condition 4: A Willingness to Commit to Using a Process Framework for School Improvement Planning and Implementation

School improvement planning is a process that involves educators in

- working together

- making decisions

- using appropriate amounts of external and internal data

- focusing on their shared agenda for change

- employing a framework that lays out the stages and steps of the overall process, such as the CREATE model

Holly and Southworth (1989) were early advocates for the production of school development plans (as they are referred to in the UK). In listing the characteristics of school development plans, they itemized ingredients that are almost axiomatic in school improvement plans today. School development plans should be

- grounded in the belief that the development of schools comes from within

- whole-school plans unifying the work of staff and students

- written in response to the views of local, regional, and central government

- written with the views of parents in mind

- in agreement with the governance board of the school

- derived from a review of current practice

- focused on needs-based priorities

School development plans should also

- have a central purpose that is expressed in terms of the improvements sought in student learning

- indicate time schedules

- identify outside help and other kinds of support activities

- analyze resource implications

- have a contractual nature (Once agreed upon by all concerned, they should be considered binding until such time as they are amended.)

This last point is an interesting one and represents something of a dilemma. What is needed, on the one hand, is a unified set of agreements to which all staff members are committed—for the long haul. On the other hand, however, as Fullan (1987) points out, what is also required is the flexible application of the plan—in the light of accumulating experience and **data**. It is a case, he says, of having to "implement the implementation plan." The balancing trick is to be able to apply the plan flexibly within parameters set by the common agreements.

Holly and Southworth (1989) also provided some practical suggestions for staff to keep in mind while working on school development plans. These are represented in the following chart.

Ten Practical Suggestions for Doing School Improvement Plans

1. Treat it as a staged process over time.

2. Record and log the various planning decisions at different stages.

3. Compile a public, shared, and negotiated document.

4. Resolve to be flexible in the implementation of the plan.

5. Link the major processes of visioning and action planning by identifying priority needs.

6. Incorporate both long-term and short-term considerations.

7. Use the process as a trigger mechanism for staff collaboration and participative decision making.

8. Separate student learning needs from staff process needs.

9. Provide a process framework and match it with appropriate techniques.

10. Use performance indicators to monitor and evaluate progress.

Pre-Conditions
Task 10: Rating Your School's Current Performance

Purpose: To rate a school's current performance in terms of quality criteria for the process of improvement planning.

<u>Grouping:</u> Work individually and then with your Learning Team.

<u>Group process strategy:</u> Use a consensus-building strategy (refer to the **Group Process Guide**).

<u>Directions:</u> Working first individually and then as a team (to come up with your consensus response), rate your school's current performance in each of the following ten areas, using a 1-5 scale with 1 being "Low" and 5 being "High."

<u>Your School's Current Performance</u>

1. School improvement planning is treated as a staged process over time.

   1   2   3   4   5

2. The various planning decisions are recorded and logged at different stages of the planning process.

   1   2   3   4   5

3. The plan, as compiled, is a public, shared, negotiated document.

   1   2   3   4   5

4. Colleagues are resolved to be flexible in implementing the plan.

   1   2   3   4   5

5. The major processes of visioning and action planning are linked by the identification of priority needs.

   1   2   3   4   5

6. The plan incorporates both long-term and short-term considerations.

   1   2   3   4   5

7. The planning process is used as a trigger mechanism for staff collaboration and participative decision making.

   1   2   3   4   5

8. The plan separates student learning needs from staff process needs.

   1   2   3   4   5

Continued

9. Staff is provided with a framework for the planning process, which is matched with appropriate techniques.

| 1 | 2 | 3 | 4 | 5 |

10. Performance indicators (success criteria) are used to monitor and evaluate the progress of the plan's implementation.

| 1 | 2 | 3 | 4 | 5 |

Looking again at the ten practical suggestions, at least four of the items refer to school improvement planning as a staged process over time. According to Holly and Southworth (1989), these process stages can be mobilized by asking trigger questions. For example:

- Where do we want to be?

- Where are we now?

- What do we need to concentrate on?

- How are we going to achieve success?

- How are we doing?

- What have we accomplished?

These six questions were used to compose the CREATE model for school improvement planning (see below). This framework is grounded in certain assumptions:

- The school improvement process is cyclical. Bellamy, Holly, and Sinisi (1997) extended this idea and introduced the concept of smaller action cycles within the larger school improvement cycle.

- The cycles are ongoing, iterative, and regenerative (see Senge, 1990).

- The cycles constitute continuous improvement as recommended by advocates of Total Quality Management (Bonstingl, 1992).

- The cycles are needs-based data-driven; continuous feedback generates further iterations of growth.

- The cycles are characterized by reflection-in-action (see Schon, 1983). Progress is continuously reviewed—as it happens.

- The cycles offer a coherent framework for school improvement.

C.R.E.A.T.E.

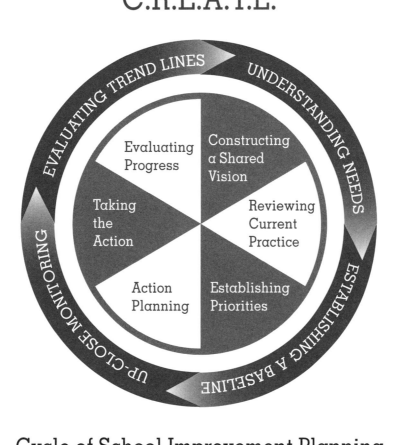

Cycle of School Improvement Planning

— Adapted from Holly and Southworth
The Developing School (1989)

The author (1990) has also itemized each stage of the school improvement planning process as follows:

<u>Stage One: Constructing a Shared Vision</u>

- Core Belief Statement

- Vision Statement

- Mission Statement

- Essential Learnings

Stage Two: Reviewing Current Practice

- Summary of Issues Arising From the Internal Data
- Summary of Messages from the External Data
- Gap Analysis/Needs Identification

Stage Three: Establishing Priorities

- Prioritizing Needs into Goals
- Creating Blended Goals

Stage Four: Action Planning

- Goal Statement
- Evaluation Plan
  - Success Criteria
  - Data Collection Techniques
  - Results Achieved
- Implementation Strategies
- Support Needs

Stage Five: Taking the Action

- Implementation Timelines, Tasks, and Responsibilities
- Staff Development
- Monitoring Implementation Efforts

Stage Six: Evaluating Progress

- Goal Achievement/Impact on Student Learning
- Effectiveness of Implementation Efforts
- Impact on Staff Climate

 Pre-Conditions ■ Task 11: Identifying Strengths and Challenges of Current Local Efforts

Purpose: To compare the six-stage school improvement process with customary practice in the participants' schools and school districts.

Grouping: Work with your Learning Team.

Group process strategy: Use the Go Round technique (refer to the **Group Process Guide**).

Directions: As a team, study the six stages of the school improvement planning process and indicate in the space below how your current local efforts match up—in terms of strengths and challenges.

Strengths	Challenges

CREATE Revisited

Now that the author has worked with the CREATE framework over several years (and has received extensive feedback on its performance), there have been four shifts in thinking. They are as follows:

1. It's a question of timing.

Completing the CREATE cycle takes more than one school year. The first two stages (visioning and data review) should take the whole of one school year when they are done thoroughly. Stages three and four (goal setting and action planning) can be done in a matter of months, but implementation, by its very nature, is a multi-year undertaking.

This is why in the *Cycles of School Improvement* (Bellamy, Holly, and Sinisi, 1997), the authors chose to use three cycles: the year-long *leadership cycle* which embraces the visioning and data review aspects; the six-month *management cycle* (goal setting and action planning); and the much shorter but multiple (mini-) *action cycles* of collaborative implementation through action research. They also emphasized that, while the first two cycles might only happen every few years, it would be the mini-action cycles that would be an ever-present, recurring feature of classrooms and schools. By the same token, schools involved in the first year of a new cycle of the North Central Association (NCA) school improvement and accreditation process are expected to gain staff commitment, identify roles and responsibilities, collect and analyze data, and develop the mission and goals. Year two is for developing the school improvement plan and year three is earmarked for beginning implementation of the plan.

In Iowa, as in many other states, all schools are currently expected to produce five-year comprehensive school improvement plans and annual progress reports. In both Dubuque and Sioux City, the schools are expected to conduct progress reviews, goal revisions—if required—and updates of their action plans on an annual basis. While these schools are still using the CREATE framework, its application is clearly not as linear as it looks on paper. In Dubuque schools, toward the end of each school year, action teams study their current data, review progress, and report to each site council. Site council members then revise the goals (if necessary), update action plans, and prepare for the next year's improvement efforts.

2. It's a question of continually learning from data.

Stage Two of the CREATE model is "Reviewing Current Practice." Originally, this was seen as the main data collection stage—tantamount to a one-time only needs assessment—out of which would spring the priority needs, which, in turn, would be translated into school improvement goals. While the needs assessment is still considered to be a valid stage in the overall cycle, it is recognized that data collection is both ongoing and continuous and accompanies (and, if used judiciously, drives) the entire school improvement process. Data use has to connect with—and replenish—all the various stages of the school improvement cycle. This is why the author (2000) now advocates for the ongoing compilation and use of a School Profile—the school's accumulating data-base for improvement planning and implementation—which can then be drawn on (like a bank account) for different purposes during the school improvement process.

In the first workbook of this series, *Conceptualizing a New Path*, it was argued that, during the process of continuous improvement, there are four stages of data collection—during which data are used to fulfill four different purposes. They include the collection of

- **needs assessment data**—in order to identify needs, establish priorities, and set goals

- **baseline data**—in order to know the current status in each goal area, prior to implementation, and to have a "yardstick" against which to measure growth over time

- **up-close data**—in order to closely monitor progress over time and to provide feedback to implementers, in the light of which they can make "in-flight" adjustments

- **trend-line data**—in order to be able to show that progress has been achieved in each of the goal areas

All of these different kinds of data can be collated into the School Profile, and when required, retrieved from the School Profile. Indeed, once in the Profile, the same data may well be used to fulfill different purposes. For instance, data that are used for the needs assessment can also provide baseline information.

3. It's a question of creating school improvement plans that are working documents.

While school improvement planning should be grounded in the broad-based involvement of various stakeholder groups, the actual written plan should be a concise, working document. It should be

- a summary of projected work (the what) and the reasons for it (the why)

- concise, yet comprehensive; slimmed down, yet substantial

- useable and, therefore, user friendly

- distributed to all invested parties—including students and their parents

- the basic script for several years of school improvement efforts

- constantly amended in the light of practice

It is its brevity that is crucial. All the major ground can be covered in a slim volume of some 20 pages (see below). This version would contain, however, only a summary of the data profile. In a style rather like students and teachers being encouraged to produce a showcase portfolio from the larger, more voluminous portfolio that is a work-in-progress, a summary school profile should focus on certain data strands which are updated annually (in order to show trend-line performance), are goal-related, and yet representative enough of the broader data base to suggest goal amendments or even the generation of new goals. Above all, the plan has to be an everyday guide to school improvement.

<u>School Improvement Plan Template</u>

Contents Page	1 page
Core Beliefs/Vision/Mission Statements	1 page
School Profile Summary	10 pages
Needs Assessment Summary	1 page
List of Priority Goals	1 page
Action Plans (one for each goal)	3 or 4 pages
Implementation Calendar (including district and building-level staff development activities)	1 page
Monitoring and Evaluation Plan	1 page
Sample Reporting Form (to be used at the end of the school year)	1 page

4. It's a case of being more accountable for fewer changes.

The more concise, useable, and focused on daily practice the plan becomes, the more it can be used for accountability purposes. There has to be accountability (for application) built into the plan. While everyone has to take responsibility for its success, words of support are not enough. As mentioned earlier, school improvement is too important to be left to chance. At Marshall Elementary School in Dubuque, for instance, a commitments sheet is used which is both a summary of all the action steps in their plan (from each of the goal areas) and a list of tasks which each staff member has to complete by the end of the year. This checklist for teacher implementation is reproduced on the next page. At Marshall School, the staff members have also made extensive use of two papers produced at the district level (which can both be found in the Appendix to the first workbook).

One paper entitled, "Implementation of the School Plan," outlines the expectations and tasks for the administration, action teams, and action team chairpersons and the other is an "Action Team Quarterly Update" sheet to be used in reporting to the school's Site Council. At Eisenhower School, in Dubuque, a faculty team built an alternative kind of commitments sheet—reproduced on the following page.

Marshall School Commitments Sheet Supporting Activities
(Teacher Based)

Language Arts

- Analyze major benchmark testing.

- Utilize ongoing evaluation to direct instruction, (e.g., Macmillan unit, mid-year).

- Provide small-group opportunities.

- Provide daily 15 minutes of "Sustained Silent Reading" and "Read Aloud."

Steps to Success® Program

- Incorporate Steps-to-Success vocabulary on a regular basis.

- Actively participate in grade-level and whole-school assemblies.

- Assist in implementation of common area plans.

Mathematics

- Analyze ITBS scores.

- Provide 5 minutes of daily fact practice time.

- Incorporate mathematics across the curriculum.

- Utilize chapter tests:

  - pre-teaching

  - re-teaching

EISENHOWER ACTION TEAM—YEARLY PLAN

School Year: _____   Action Team: _____

Members: _____

_____

_____

District/School Goal: _____

_____

Activities	How will the activity be accomplished?	Who will be responsible for the activity?	Describe the necessary resources (time & materials, such as substitutes)	What is the targeted date for completion?	What data will indicate success of this goal?

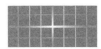 Pre-Conditions
Task 12: Designing Commitments Sheets

<u>Purpose:</u> To produce commitments sheets that can be used in the participants' schools for accountability purposes.

<u>Grouping:</u> Work as a school team.

<u>Directions:</u> Working as a school team, use the example materials to design a school improvement commitments sheet that could be used by all staff members in your school.

School Improvement Commitments Sheet

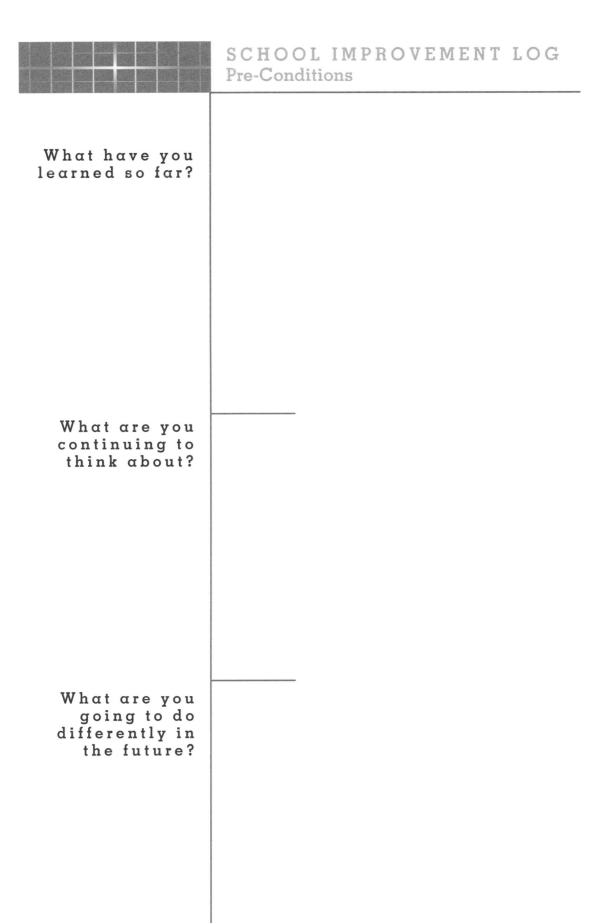

What have you learned so far?

What are you continuing to think about?

What are you going to do differently in the future?

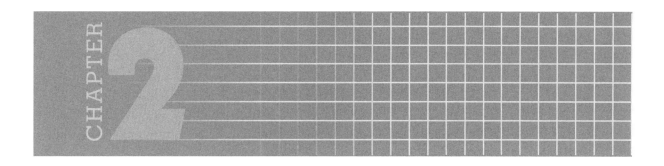

CHAPTER TWO: THE SCHOOL IMPROVEMENT PROCESS

■ Each of the six stages of the CREATE school improvement process is a separate part of Chapter Two of this workbook.

■ There are three themes running through each part:

   ■ a commentary that is a description of the stage itself

   ■ a set of sample techniques, tools, and activities that can be used to activate the stage

   ■ practical suggestions about how data can be used at this stage of school improvement

C.R.E.A.T.E.

Cycle of School Improvement Planning

— Adapted from Holly and Southworth
The Developing School (1989)

The Six Stages of the CREATE School Improvement Process

<u>Stage One: Constructing a Shared Vision</u>

- Core Belief Statement

- Vision Statement

- Mission Statement

- Essential Learnings

<u>Stage Two: Reviewing Current Practice</u>

- Summary of Issues Arising From the Internal Data

- Summary of Messages from the External Data

- Gap Analysis/Needs Identification

<u>Stage Three: Establishing Priorities</u>

- Prioritizing Needs into Goals

- Creating Blended Goals

<u>Stage Four: Action Planning</u>

- Goal Statement

- Evaluation Plan

- Implementation Strategies

- Support Needs

<u>Stage Five: Taking the Action</u>

- Implementation Timelines, Tasks, and Responsibilities

- Staff Development

- Monitoring Implementation Efforts

<u>Stage Six: Evaluating Progress</u>

- Goal Achievement/Impact on Student Learning

- Effectiveness of Implementation Efforts

- Impact on Staff Climate

STAGE 1

Constructing a Shared Vision

Overview

The task at this first stage of school improvement is to do exactly as the title says—to create a view of the school's future that is shared by enough members of enough important stakeholder groups. What this suggests immediately is that a shared vision emerges from a shared visioning process. What this also means is that the responsibility of school leaders is not to come up with the vision (although they should certainly contribute their ideas), but to create the process conditions where a shared vision can be generated. Peter Senge (1990) has written cogently on this issue as follows:

> Today, 'vision' is a familiar concept in corporate leadership. But when you look carefully you will find that most 'visions' are one person's (or one group's) vision imposed on an organization. Such visions, at best, command compliance—not commitment. A shared vision is a vision that many people are truly committed to, because it reflects their own personal vision....When people truly share a vision they are connected, bound together by a common aspiration.

Paraphrasing Senge's other advice, a shared vision is

- the answer to the question, "What do we want to create?"

- a picture of the future that is carried in the hearts and minds of people in the organization

- something that is palpable, not an abstraction (People can see it, sense it, almost touch it.)

- the source of a sense of commonality and loyalty that permeates the organization and gives coherence to diverse activities (It is the iron hoop around the barrel.)

- inspiring and compelling, exhilarating and uplifting of people's aspirations (It is the spark, says Senge, that lifts an organization out of the mundane.)

- "ours" not "theirs" (It changes people's relationships with an organization; it creates a common identity, a shared sense of purpose and operating values.)

- what forces our planning efforts to be more than just short term and reactive

No wonder that schools and school districts are encouraged, every several years, to take the time to create and realize the power of shared visions. Done well, so much can flow from such an endeavor. Richardson (1996) emphasizes that powerful words can energize schools and school districts to see what direction they're going and what they will look like when they arrive at their destination. She continues:

> Vision and mission statements can focus schools by assisting all elements of a community in knowing what they're all about. They're devices that schools can use to steer them in the right direction.

While vision and mission statements are both important, she says, they are different and serve different purposes.

> In a nutshell, a vision statement is a picture of what you want your school or district to look like at a certain point in time. A mission statement is a more action-oriented description of what must be done to create that vision.

In order to draw out the difference between the two kinds of statements, Richardson cites Susan Everson's apt metaphor of a couple wanting to give a dinner party. Their mission is to do everything they can to have a successful event; their vision is their picture-in-mind of what the dinner should look like. As Everson observes, if they don't have the same picture-in-mind, the dinner party could prove a disaster. They could be working completely at odds with each other.

A Shared Vision: Three Key Points

A vision should be shared and future-oriented. It should also have three other characteristics. First, **the vision should look ten to fifteen years into the future.** If the view is more short-term than that, the horizon is lowered, the challenge is lessened, and the temptation is to remain in the present. As Senge (1990) has said, the vision has to produce enough creative tension between the now and the projected then to generate a will for change. If the vision looks more than fifteen years into the future, however, it ceases to have any meaning; it becomes too abstract and too irrelevant.

Second, **the vision should be values-based.** A vision should entail the elaboration of our core values and beliefs in a future-oriented action setting. Argyris and Schon (1978) made a distinction between our espoused values (what we say we value) and our values-in-use (what our daily practice demonstrates we value). In terms of the enactment of a vision, there should be no distinction: our values-in-use should be our espoused values. The question to ask, therefore, is, "What would it look like if our core values and beliefs were being practiced on a daily basis?"

Third, and extending this second point, **the vision and the core values that underpin it have to be lived and breathed**. The written documents have to leap off the page and the statements come alive. Collins (1996), referring to the business world, has warned of the dangers of putting too much attention on the written words and not enough emphasis on their implementation.

> Executives spend too much time drafting, word-smithing, and redrafting vision statements, mission statements, values statements, purpose statements, aspiration statements, and so on. They spend nowhere near enough time trying to align their organizations with the values and visions already in place.

The process of alignment is more important than coming up with the perfect statement. It is certainly not a waste of time, he says, to think through fundamental questions like, "What are our core values?" and "What do we aspire to achieve and become?" While emphasizing the importance of visions, Collins says they have three elements: the organization's reasons for existence, its timeless, unchanging core values, and the "huge and audacious aspirations" for the future. But, in his mind, it is the alignment question that is all-important. There should be as much congruence as possible between values and practice, vision and performance. Indeed, he says:

> When you have superb alignment, a visitor could drop into your organization from another planet and infer the vision without having to read it on paper.

 Constructing a Shared Vision
Task 1: Reflecting on Reading

<u>Purpose:</u> To encourage small-group reflection on the content of the Overview.

<u>Grouping:</u> Work individually and then in pairs.

<u>Group process strategy:</u> Use the Three-Step Interview.

<u>Directions:</u> Working individually, respond to this commentary by answering the following questions. Then, share your responses with your Learning Team colleagues using the three-step interview.

- Which points raised in the commentary do you agree with and why?

- Which points do you disagree with and why?

- What has challenged your thinking?

Creating a Shared Vision—Some Useful Definitions

Core Beliefs

These are the fundamental beliefs, values, and principles that we hold dear. We feel most satisfied and fulfilled when our core beliefs drive all our actions.

Vision

This is a picture-in-words, which describes what life would be like if the core beliefs and actions were in harmony. The vision describes this future state—what it would look like, sound like, and feel like.

Mission

This is a brief statement (probably 30 words or less) that summarizes the role of a particular group or organization in realizing the vision.

Essential Learnings

These are the cross-curricular learning experiences that you want all students to receive and the attributes and skills that all students should acquire as a result of having these experiences.

Goals

These are the focus areas that are chosen by a group or organization as the particular roads to travel in realizing its mission. Goals provide specific direction and help us move from where we are now (the current reality) to where we want to be (the vision).

Constructing a Shared Vision
Task 2: Evaluating Your Current School Vision

<u>Purpose:</u> To evaluate the existing vision prior to its renewal/regeneration.

<u>Grouping:</u> Work individually and then with your Learning Team.

<u>Group process strategy:</u> Use a consensus-building strategy (refer to the **Group Process Guide**) to reach a consensus score for each statement.

<u>Directions:</u> Working individually and then coming together as a team to reach consensus, evaluate your current school vision by rating each of the following twelve statements on a 1-5 scale, with 1 being "Strongly Disagree" to 5 being "Strongly Agree." For instance, if you think that your school's/school district's vision is *somewhat* shared by all stakeholder groups, you might choose to give this statement a rating of "3" on the scale, while if you think—in response to another statement—that the vision has minimal impact on classroom practice, you would might rate this statement as a "1." When the consensus score for each statement has been agreed upon, tally the scores of all the statements to obtain a total score.

Enter the Total Score here: _____

<u>Please Note</u>

If the total score is in the 50-60 range: Celebrate! Your vision has great power.

If the total score is in the 30-40 range: Think! Your vision has some merits, but, equally, there are some concerns.

If the total score is below 25: Reach for your calendar! You need to book a visioning session.

Evaluating Your School's Existing Vision

My school has an existing vision.

1	2	3	4	5

Strongly Disagree   Strongly Agree

I know what is in the existing vision.

1	2	3	4	5

The vision is widely shared.

1	2	3	4	5

The vision is futuristic and visionary.

1	2	3	4	5

The vision is written in powerful, evocative language.

1	2	3	4	5

The vision is still current and has not passed its "sell-date."

1	2	3	4	5

There has been minimal staff turnover since the vision was created.

1	2	3	4	5

Staff members are still committed to its realization.

1	2	3	4	5

The vision is often mentioned, honored, and celebrated.

1	2	3	4	5

The vision guides daily practice in our school and classrooms.

1	2	3	4	5

The vision is articulated in various written statements, such as core beliefs, vision statements, and mission statements.

1	2	3	4	5

There are parts of the existing statements that deserve to be retained for their power, meaningfulness, and relevance.

1	2	3	4	5

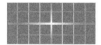 Constructing a Shared Vision
Task 3: Identifying Concerns and Actions

<u>Purpose:</u> To begin to identify concerns regarding the current vision and the remedial actions that are required.

<u>Grouping:</u> Work with your Learning Team.

<u>Directions:</u> If concerns were identified during the process of evaluating your school's vision, list them below along with possible remedial actions.

Concerns	Actions

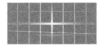

Constructing a Shared Vision
Task 4: Creating Vision and Mission Statements

Purpose: To construct shared vision and mission statements that are grounded in core beliefs.

Grouping: Work individually, in small groups, and then as a whole staff. A group reporter should be selected to share group work with the whole group.

Directions: This major task has been designed as a process for school faculties (working individually, in small groups, and as a whole staff) to use to generate a Statement of Core Beliefs, a Vision Statement, and a Mission Statement. The process is in five steps that, if scheduled together during an in-service session, would take between two and a half to three hours to complete. If you are using this workbook as a small team, the process instructions remain the same. You would not, however, include Step Three—the whole group (faculty) sharing.

Step One: Individual Reflection

From your personal standpoint, please complete each statement below regarding your TOP TEN CORE BELIEFS concerning the components of an effective education.

1. I believe that _____

2. I believe that _____

3. I believe that _____

4. I believe that _____

5. I believe that _____

6. I believe that _____

7. I believe that _____

8. I believe that _____

9. I believe that _____

10. I believe that _____

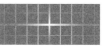

Step Two: Group Work

Having produced your individual lists, the task is now to combine them to the satisfaction of the group members. Using the chart below, place your items into three categories:

1. Those items that are repeated across the individual lists and can, therefore, easily be placed on a combined list. They are the "Definites."

2. Those items that may well be saying the same thing but you are not absolutely sure. They are the "Maybes."

3. Those items that do not correspond with any other items on the other lists. They are the "Singles."

DEFINITES	MAYBES	SINGLES

Step Three: Whole-Group Sharing

Step Two is then repeated for the whole group, with each group's reporter sharing the group's "Definites," "Maybes," and "Singles." The purpose is to find ten core beliefs that are cherished by the whole group.

Note: A whole-group recorder should be selected to record each group's "Definites" on a wall chart.

Step Four: Drawing the Vision Together

A vision is a picture-in-words of the core beliefs in action. So now take your newly modeled core belief statement and translate it into a word picture. Describe what you would see, hear, and feel if you walked into your school in the future and saw the core beliefs in action. You may choose to do this first as an individual, pairs, or small group activity, and then as a whole-group activity.

Step Five: Writing a Mission Statement

Using the "Pruning" Technique

As a whole group, scan all the completed work and select key words and ideas that suggest what has to be done to accomplish your core beliefs and vision. For example, if one of the core beliefs is "all students can learn," someone (or some group) has to make this happen. Then, assemble the key words and ideas in a paragraph of continuous prose, but not using more than 30 words. Remember that the finished product should be brief and summarize the role and responsibilities of a particular group or organization in realizing the vision.

Note: A facilitator/recorder should be selected to implement this step with the whole group.

Generating Essential Learnings

This important task can be completed in a number of ways; two sample processes are outlined below. The importance of Essential Learnings is underlined in the first workbook in this series, *Conceptualizing a New Path*. What needs emphasizing here is that Essential Learnings are the vital link between the core beliefs and vision statements and the everyday world of classroom practice. Essential Learnings are for all students and are often written as exit-level performance standards (see the example from Sioux City, Iowa on the next page) or as graduation requirements. They also tend to define the horizontal curriculum—what has to happen in every subject area across the curriculum.

<u>Sample Process #1</u>

"Backward Mapping" is a small-group process (that can lead to whole-group sharing) in which the participants create Essential Learnings and a supportive context for their accomplishment by brainstorming group responses to four trigger questions:

Question One: What should we be striving to achieve with our students?
(The answers will define the Essential Learnings.)

Question Two: What should the classroom as a learning center be like in order to accomplish the Essential Learnings?

Question Three: What should the school as a learning organization be like in order to support the classroom as a learning center?

Question Four: What should the district as a learning community be like in order to support the school as a learning organization?

Sioux City Community School District
Exit-Level Performance Standards

As a result of their education, all graduates will be

1. **Fluent Communicators** who listen and respond to others' messages and ideas, who create original ideas and relate information in various contexts, and who demonstrate fluency in written and oral form.

2. **Collaborative Individuals** who use skillful leadership and responsible social and group skills to develop and manage interpersonal relationships within culturally and organizationally diverse settings.

3. **Problem Solvers** who identify problems, use strategies to approach problems, and apply mathematical, logical, and creative reasoning to solve problems and make appropriate decisions.

4. **Technological Practitioners** who use advanced technologies, including but not limited to the computer, to create, access, integrate, and use information to communicate, reason, make decisions, and solve complex problems in a variety of contexts.

5. **Resourceful Learners** who create a positive vision for themselves and their future, view themselves as lifelong learners, set priorities and achievable goals, create options for themselves, monitor and evaluate their progress, and assume responsibility for their actions.

6. **Quality Workers** who create and appreciate intellectual, artistic, practical, and physical products which reflect originality, high standards, and the use of advanced technology.

7. **Life Managers** who demonstrate the motivation and skills necessary to preserve and make wise decisions which reflect healthful living, interdependence, and ethical behavior that contribute to society.

<u>Sample Process #2</u>

This process involves translating Core Beliefs into Essential Learnings. Take for instance this set of Core Beliefs:

- All students can learn.

- Students learn best actively—not passively.

- Learners will construct their own knowledge—grounded in what they already know.

- Everyone has a right to be treated with dignity and respect.

- Social and emotional safety is a necessary context for learning.

- Engagement comes only with the belief in the authenticity of the learning.

- Success breeds success—our job is to engineer the first successes.

- Reading is a gateway skill.

- Reading, mathematics, and technology skills are the basic skills of the future.

- Working with others to accomplish meaningful tasks is the primary employability skill.

The task now is to look down this list and see which of these Core Belief statements can be translated into Essential Learnings. Some Core Beliefs may speak to teaching and teachers only (e.g., "our job is to engineer the first successes"), while others may speak directly to student learning. It is the latter that will be most easily translated into Essential Learnings (what students need to know and be able to do). Using the Core Beliefs from above, the following list of Essential Learnings emerges:

This district believes it is essential that students

- have successful learning experiences

- actively work with and construct their own knowledge

- treat each other with respect and dignity as responsible members of a global society

- engage in authentic learning experiences

- demonstrate competency in reading

- work collaboratively

- acquire reading, mathematics, and technology skills

 ## Constructing a Shared Vision
Task 5: Translating Core Beliefs Into Essential Learnings

Purpose: To translate core beliefs into essential learnings so that what has been agreed upon at the organizational level can begin to impact what happens on a daily basis at the classroom level.

Grouping: Work with your Learning Team.

Directions: Working as a team, take the Core Beliefs that you generated in Task 4 and translate them—if possible—into a set of Essential Learnings for your school/school district.

The Role of Data in Creating a Shared Vision

The role of data in the shared visioning process might not be as obvious as in other stages of the school improvement cycle, but, nevertheless, it is just as important. These, however, are not the usual kinds of data. They are ideas, concepts, thoughts, and insights about the future; they are not "facts." They are discovered and articulated by insiders, but they come from the outside. They are external data, which are the kind of data that suggest other possibilities, other potentialities. It is external data that can help us anticipate the future. Indeed, by means of an extensive "environmental scanning" of the available external data, it becomes possible to identify the major social and economic trends that should be taken into account when becoming involved in a visioning process.

Any scanning of social and economic trends over the last ten years would have produced much of the same kinds of lists of issues. These issues would include:

- a rapidly changing—and expanding—knowledge base

- new technologies in all areas of life

- instant worldwide communication

- increasing international interdependence on one hand and more accentuated localism on the other

- a shift from a manufacturing to a service economy

- frequent changes in the workplace

- an increasingly diverse population

- changes in personal and family roles

- an aging population

- an increasing emphasis on health and wellness

This list, however, is already somewhat out-of-date. There is no mention of several crucial issues, including school security and safety, economic turbulence and the downturn in the fortunes of the stock market, increased patriotism and the war against terrorism, and the threat posed by global warming.

It is interesting to look at John Naisbitt's *Megatrends* books and see how much his forecasts have proven right or wrong. His first book (published in 1982) predicts shifts from

- Industrial Society —> to Information Society

- Forced Technology —> to High Tech/High Touch

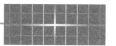

- National Economy —> to World Economy

- Short Term —> to Long Term

- Centralization —> to Decentralization

- Institutional Help —> Self-Help

- Representative Democracy —> to Participative Democracy

- Hierarchies —> to Networking

- North —> to South

- Either/or —> to Multiple Options

His second book (co-authored with Patricia Aburdene, 1990) lists several different trends:

- Booming Global Economy of 1990s

- Renaissance in the Arts

- Emergence of Free-Market Socialism

- Global Lifestyles and Cultural Nationalism

- Privatization of the Welfare State

- Rise of the Pacific Rim

- Decade of Women in Leadership

- The Age of Biology

- Religious Revival

- Triumph of the Individual

His trend analysis is good but not perfect. Anticipating the future is not an exact science. It will be interesting to see if the explosion of information on the Internet makes trend analysis any more reliable.

While visioning is dependent on the application of new, fresh, and stimulating ideas, processing strategies are required to transform such disparate information from diverse people into a common agenda.

Future Search: A Collaborative Visioning Process

Weisbord and Janoff (1995) introduced the concept of a "Future Search"—a large group planning meeting that brings the community into the room to work on a task-focused agenda. According to the authors:

> The meeting is based on a simple notion: if we want dramatic new action plans, we need to use structures and processes congruent with our aspirations. Such aspirations—sometimes labeled 'cultural transformation' or 'paradigm shift'—seem abstract, elusive, and hard to initiate. They can, however, be experienced and used to practical advantage by those willing to work under a set of conditions.

Those involved in a "Future Search" meeting experience a five-step process. They take joint action toward a desired future by

- reviewing the past

- exploring the present

- creating ideal future scenarios

- identifying common ground

- making action plans

Above all, say Weisbord and Janoff, participants leap into uncharted territory and, through open dialogue, work toward the discovery and use of a common agenda—but not an agenda held by any individuals when they entered the room. The final agenda—the common ground—emerges from the group interaction.

An Example Topic for a Future Search

Under the title "The Kids in Our Community—Where are We Going?" participants could begin by studying the kinds of data contained in "Kids These Days 1999: What Americans Really Think About the Next Generation," a Public Agenda report (1999):

Finding One: Negative reactions

- Most Americans describe children and teens in negative terms.

- Neither adults nor teens believe the next generation will make America a better place.

Finding Two: A focus on values and respect

- Not learning values tops the public's list of problems facing kids.

- It's not very common to come across friendly, helpful, respectful young people.

Finding Three: Putting the blame on parents

- Americans think too many parents fail to do their job.

- Today, more Americans blame irresponsible parents rather than economic pressures for the problems kids face.

Finding Four: Difficult circumstances

- People believe it's harder to be a parent today.

- People also recognize that kids face many dangers and temptations.

Finding Five: Little willingness to write off kids

- Americans say helping kids is a top priority.

- And they believe even the most troubled youngsters can be reached.

Finding Six: The role of government

- People support solutions close to home.

- Few people see a shortage of government programs as a very serious problem for kids.

Finding Seven: Positive attitudes among teens

- The news from teenagers is good (they trust their parents to be there when needed, have other adults to talk to, have faith in God, and trust their friends to be there).

- But they have plenty of time on their hands to go astray.

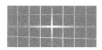 Constructing a Shared Vision
Task 6: Conducting a Local Future Search

Purpose: To take the idea of a Future Search and apply it to the participants' local contexts.

Grouping: Work with your Learning Team.

Directions: Discuss in your team how a community-based Future Search could be conducted in your local community, perhaps using the example topic and the research findings as outlined in the last section. Who would need to be involved? How could it be organized? What could it aim to achieve?

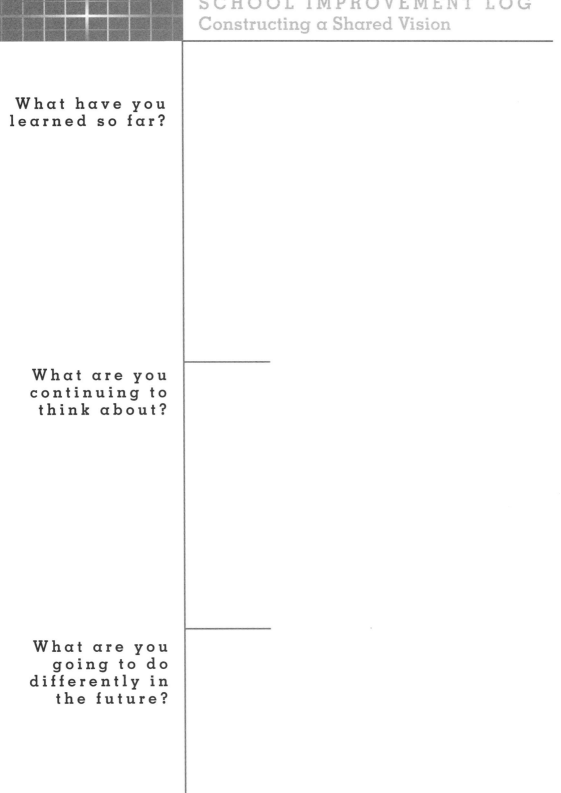

**What have you
learned so far?**

**What are you
continuing to
think about?**

**What are you
going to do
differently in
the future?**

Notes

54

Stage 2

Reviewing Current Practice

Overview

This second stage of the school improvement cycle is when the process genuinely becomes needs-based data-driven. This is when mainly internal data are studied for the purposes of a needs assessment. Studying the available data uncovers the following:

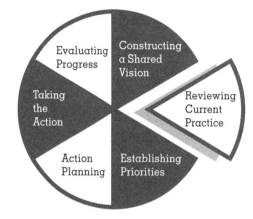

- The issues, problems, and concerns that are recurring throughout the different kinds of data.

- The challenges (which are often received in the form of negative responses) as well as the strengths (positive responses).

- The largest and the most significant gaps and discrepancies between where we want to be (the vision) and where we are now (the current reality). These are the priority areas that are demanding focused and sustained attention. This major task of setting the data concerning the current reality against the already established shared vision, according to Senge (1990), is what energizes the improvement process.

Charting the current reality has several consequences, as follow:

- Awareness is raised, assumptions are challenged, and, according to Festinger (1954), cognitive dissonance is generated. Having our eyes opened in this way can be disconcerting, discomforting, even alarming. Creative tension is provoked between our hearts and our brains; we want to keep thinking one way, but the data is informing our minds otherwise. We have to "Mind the Gap" (between our vision and core beliefs and what the data is telling us is actually the case) as illustrated below.

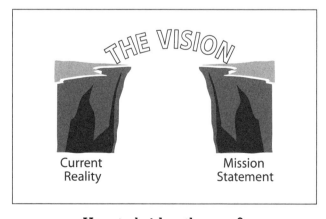

How to bridge the gap?

■ Strengths on which to build are discovered and needs (areas where we need to get stronger) identified. This approach is sometimes criticized for being a "deficiency model," a criticism that is somewhat perplexing. In this process, strengths are recognized, celebrated and capitalized upon. Indeed, in the experience of this author, we are much more likely to respond to negative feedback if, simultaneously, we are being provided with positive endorsements. It's the psychology of change at work. Yet, naturally enough, it is our needs that are given the most attention—because we need to attend to them!

■ Needs assessment data can also be recycled—at the action planning stage—to provide baseline data concerning the current status in each of the selected goal areas.

The North Central Association (NCA) accreditation process has long included a needs assessment and participants are provided with advice about how to proceed with this important stage. In terms of an overview, participants are informed as follows:

> Needs assessment is the process of gathering, analyzing, and evaluating information about the differences between conditions as they currently exist and ones that are more desirable. Needs may result from significant problems or may simply represent conditions which are considered better. Needs may also emerge from the development of a vision of where a school wants to be at some point in the future. The result of an assessment should be a set of clearly articulated goals to meet the needs or solve the problems identified.
>
> However, care must be taken when assembling and using data generated by a needs assessment. Too often, assessment means a quick and superficial written survey. In other cases, a needs assessment is overdone and turns into a laborious, lengthy process that exhausts everyone's energy and time. There must be a balance between the typical quick and superficial assessment and an in-depth, exhaustive one that depletes time and energy.

The same NCA guidance material contains a "Summary of Best Practices in (Needs) Assessment" (National Inservice Network, 1980):

■ Needs assessment should be a conscious public activity that draws on the internal knowledge of staff as well as the external knowledge base about effective teaching and learning.

- Needs assessment should be an ongoing process, starting more generically and, as awareness grows, becoming more specific.

- Staff perceptions about their own needs must be viewed as important, as must staff participation in the needs assessment process itself. Inclusion in the needs assessment means that staff can take responsibility for assessing their own needs, as well as the needs of others, and the process itself becomes educational and part of staff development.

- Needs should be individualized by building—given the uniqueness of each school and its needs.

- Needs assessment information should be gathered from one source, using different data collection techniques and thus adding to the validity and legitimacy of the process.

- An analysis should also be made of the strengths of the system, thus maintaining a balanced perspective and bolstering confidence.

- There must be a visible relationship between the needs assessment and the program delivered. Participation in needs identification creates expectations that services—to meet the needs—will be provided.

This good advice for NCA schools touches on four key understandings:

1. While a needs assessment employs largely internal data (data that speak to the internal condition of the school), external data also come into play. Consideration of data from the external knowledge base reveals generic needs—needs pertaining to all schools. Indeed, it is often the "big issues" (e.g., equity, diversity, excellence, and so on) that emerge from such a wide study. Participants read or hear about "conditions which are considered better" or are alerted to problems that are generic across all schools (e.g., school safety and violence).

2. In a needs assessment there is an important balance to be struck between studying enough data from a wide variety of sources and conserving both time and energy.

3. While comprehensive coverage is provided, the aim is to traverse from breadth to specificity. It's a case of broadening out to be able to focus down, casting a wide enough net to catch the important fish.

4. The needs assessment process is a golden opportunity to involve those who will be charged with program implementation in identifying the very issues and concerns that give rise to the need for the program. "Identification of" leads to "identification with." Ownership of and investment in the issues are crucial if staff members are to commit to sustained implementation efforts.

Provided below is an example of how the public, open scrutiny of data can "unfreeze" attitudes and assumptions and unlock the door to change.

Putting a "School-to-Work"

In a particular high school, with which the author has worked, the majority of faculty members were in denial about the need for a school-to-work program. State and federal funds were available and the district's curriculum director wrote a successful grant application. Yet nothing happened. Then a one-day session was organized for staff to look at their internal data (as part of their NCA needs assessment) and identify their school improvement needs. The day was organized very carefully. What occurred had to be organized well, but not stage-managed in any manipulative sense. Using an open, public process similar to the "data carousel" suggested by Holcomb (1999), all staff members, working in small groups, scrutinized the various kinds of data available—including, crucially, student and graduate feedback data—and sought common-ground findings, using the Tambourine method described in the **Group Process Guide**. By the end of the afternoon, when all the small groups reported out, it became eminently clear that the faculty had "discovered'" school-to-work, almost as their own invention. Each group report mentioned this particular need—as though it had never been mentioned before. They had constructed the "why" and the need was lodged in the hearts and minds of the participants. Interestingly, several years on, this school is seen as one of the shining lights for school-to-work endeavors across the state.

Reviewing Current Practice
Task 1: Unblocking Resistance to Change

<u>Purpose:</u> To reflect on previous experiences where scrutinizing data unblocked resistance to the possibility of change.

<u>Grouping:</u> Work individually and then share with your Learning Team.

<u>Group processing strategy:</u> Use the Turn to Your Partner technique found in the **Group Process Guide**.

<u>Directions:</u> Working individually, write an account of a similar occasion from your own experience. Was it successful or unsuccessful and why or why not? What could have been done differently? Share your experience with a partner using Turn to Your Partner.

The School Profile

Chapter One of this workbook contained the argument that the data for a needs assessment should be drawn from the School Profile, a standing and accumulating collection of data that can be used for several purposes during the process of school improvement. Such a data bank, if well maintained over time, should have all the necessary data in an easily retrievable form. Such a collection of data is sometimes referred to as a School Portfolio. While the fifth book in this series of workbooks, *Creating a Data-Driven System*, focuses on the use of profiles in schools and school districts, what should be explained now is that the School Profile

- is a cumulative data-base

- is organized using a comprehensive framework from which can be drawn data for use in

  - assessing needs, deciding priorities, and setting goals

  - reporting annually

  - monitoring progress in each goal area and showing growth over time

  - updating long-range plans

- is a kind of data bank account into which deposits—and from which withdrawals—can be made and where such transactions are ongoing and continuous

- should be constantly in use; it is a living, breathing organism

Practical Purposes of the School Profile:

- reporting to the district and the state

- comparing progress with other schools in the district

- developing a needs assessment

- writing annual reports

- writing grant applications

- reporting to parents

- reporting to the community

- writing and updating school improvement plans

- writing a school brochure

- sharing with prospective teachers

- sharing with visitors and prospective parents

- developing a school report card

Given the *No Child Left Behind* federal legislation and its emphasis on schools and school districts having to track the progress of all students (and all sub-populations of students) in data over time, the need for the establishment and maintenance of high quality School Profiles is becoming widely recognized. The next challenge is to come up with electronic School Profiles or Portfolios that facilitate the process of data storage and retrieval. This topic will be explored in the fifth workbook in this series.

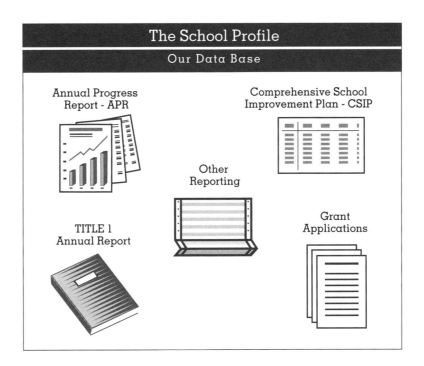

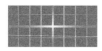 **Reviewing Current Practice**
Task 2: Using Data Profiles

Purpose: To ascertain whether data profiles are currently being used and, if not, how the participants could go about creating them.

Grouping: Work with your Learning Team.

Directions: As a team, discuss whether your school has such a data profile.

Yes _____ No _____

If your answer is "yes," discuss the status and ingredients of your profile. What needs to be added or deleted?

If your answer is "no," discuss how you could begin to put one together. What should be included?

Record your ideas below.

In Dubuque Schools (Dubuque, Iowa), the School Profile is used on an annual basis to look back and look forward. It contains a progress review of the previous school improvement efforts and a new, revised plan grounded in a scrutiny of the current data base.

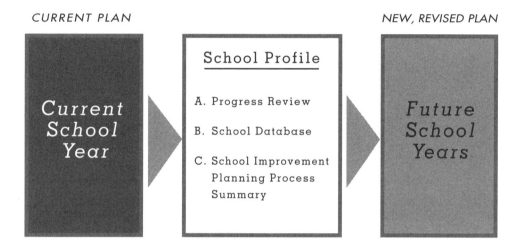

CURRENT PLAN

NEW, REVISED PLAN

Current School Year

School Profile

A. Progress Review

B. School Database

C. School Improvement Planning Process Summary

Future School Years

Developing A School Profile

The North Central Association (NCA) has published an excellent handbook to assist schools in the development of a School Profile entitled *Developing the School Profile. A Handbook for Schools* (NCA, 2000). The introduction contains the following advice:

> The school profile is a concise stand-alone document developed to summarize information that describes the students within a specific school. To be useful the focus must be on community, student, and instructional characteristics that are relevant to student performance and school improvement.
>
> The profile enables the community to identify student strengths and needs. It is the document from which student performance goals emerge. As such, the profile provides baseline information relative to student performance that can be used later for comparisons when determining the success of the school's improvement plan.

This stand-alone document should have the following characteristics:

- Relatively brief—not pages of data.

- Appropriate analysis of data—not lengthy descriptions of data.

- Data that are important to know vs. data that are nice to know.

- Data developed and presented to be understood by the average person.

- Data presented in charts, graphs, and other pictorial representations.

- Succinct analysis of data to provide interpretations of findings. (What do these data mean?)

The School Profile is written by faculty members for faculty members. Information needs to be displayed in a format that will be readily usable by the faculty members. Therefore, all parts of the profile should be shared and discussed by faculty. The goal of the document is to provide a picture of what is taking place in the school in terms of teaching and learning.

REMEMBER! Bigger is not better! The task is to select, consolidate, and display the most useful information relative to student performance. Users of the profile should not be expected to wade through stacks of computer-generated output.

As suggested in the introduction to this workbook, the School Profile should be a summary document that becomes part of the school improvement plan. Like a student's showcase portfolio, this summary is a faithful representation of a much larger body of data that is contained in the school's data base—the working documentation from which the summary document is drawn.

The NCA guidance material also provides an outline framework for the contents of a School Profile:

> Cover Page
>
> Table of Contents
>
> School Mission (Vision) Statement
>
> Data

The data section is in three parts:

> **Unique Local Insights:** display of information collected from questionnaires, surveys, "opinionnaires," and/or interviews from people who know the school best
>
> **Follow-up of Former Students:** graduates, student dropouts; reports from students, receiving teachers (e.g., middle school, high school, and colleges) as well as employers
>
> **Existing School Data:** information already in the school data base related to students, instruction, and community

The School Profile in Action

In Dubuque Schools, the concept of a School Profile has been implemented in each of the twenty buildings across the district—largely along the lines suggested by the NCA guidance materials. During Data Coach training sessions the following framework was presented (Holly and Lange, 2001) for the purposes of "Needs Assessment Using an NCA-Type School Profile:"

Core Component 1: Unique Local Insights

<u>Purpose</u>

Local insights from the total school community (faculty, staff, administration, students, parents, business and community leaders, and so on) provide perspectives on the strengths and challenges of the schooling process from those who know the school best. Perception data are the requirement here.

<u>Methods</u>

Data collection using questionnaires, surveys, (including customer satisfaction and climate surveys), focus groups, and interviews with key stakeholders.

Core Component 2: Follow-up of Former Students

Purpose

Reporting on the progress of former students by connecting with five important groups of respondents:

- Graduates themselves (including those from elementary and middle schools); they can speak from experience in terms of the school-related strengths and deficiencies in their academic preparation.

- Promoted students; they can provide information concerning the degree of their preparedness for the next level of their education.

- Student dropouts; they can help with a careful examination of the causes of their departure and its relatedness to prior academic performance.

- Teachers and parents; they have perceptions based on their continuing (more informal) connections with the students.

- Receiving teachers (an important, under-used group) have the advantage of being able to compare the skill level of the new batch of students with that of previous groups.

- University teachers and employers who can speak to the skill levels of the young people entering their establishments.

Methods

Data collection using telephone interviews (selected by random sampling), face-to-face interviews, and questionnaires.

Core Component 3: Existing School Data

Purpose

Already existing data can be retrieved to show changes in performance levels over time. Trend analysis can be conducted using student, instructional, and community data and disaggregation used to reveal inequalities and discrepancies between various client groups.

Based on the NCA advice, the following **student data** are collated and studied in Dubuque:

- enrollment/class size

- attendance and tardiness

- retention rates

■ discrimination and harassment reports

■ discipline referrals

■ suspensions and expulsions

■ dropout rates

■ graduation rates

■ achievement and failure patterns across grade levels

■ standardized test scores, including the percentage of students at the low, intermediate, and high performance levels in reading and mathematics in grades 4, 8, and 11, plus science and social studies in grades 8 and 11.

■ other school-wide assessments

■ stability/mobility of students

■ co-curricular participation rates

Student data is disaggregated with the following factors in mind:

■ special education/individualized education plans (IEPs)

■ race/ethnicity

■ gender

■ socioeconomic status

■ Title 1

■ vocational education

■ ESL/migrant/bilingual

■ family structure (including homeless)

■ employment status

■ transience

■ length of time in the district

■ at-risk

■ extracurricular activity participants

Instructional data include the following:

- instructional characteristics, including the most commonly used instructional techniques

- number of sections and full-time employment (FTE) of teachers per grade level or department

- student-engaged time

- staff development opportunities

- school organization and schedule

- support programs

- external research and professional literature currently being studied for its relevance to school improvement

Community data include the following:

- local, state, and federal mandates that impact the school program

- community programs/facilities

- school-business partnerships

- state/national/international trends and their implications

- recent community demographic changes (in the school's catchment area)

- parent and community organizations that encourage and support the school

- community attitudes towards learning

- avenues of input to the district/school for community stakeholder groups

<u>Methods</u>

These existing data largely consist of documentation and records that can be stored in the school's data base. The important task here is to be able to summarize these data and present them in easily digested formats (such as charts, graphs, or tables) that show trends and growth over time.

In Dubuque, a self-assessment tool (see the following pages) has been used to identify the schools' needs relative to the collection and collation of these data.

 Reviewing Current Practice
Task 3: Using a Self-Assessment Instrument

Purpose: To use a self-assessment instrument that denotes the current availability of various kinds of data for inclusion in the School Profile.

Grouping: Work with your Learning Team.

Directions: Working as a team, complete the following self-assessment instrument (compiled by the author's colleague, Mary Lange) in order to review the current status of data availability in your school/school district.

CHECKLIST OF CURRENTLY AVAILABLE AND COLLECTED DATA

Data Source	Currently in School Data	Needs to be collected	Responsibility Who?	When?
Unique Local Insights: perspectives on the strengths and weaknesses of the schooling process from the perceptions of…				
Faculty	☐	☐		
Staff	☐	☐		
Administration	☐	☐		
Students	☐	☐		
Parents	☐	☐		
Business and community leaders	☐	☐		
Other aspects of the school community that identify its uniqueness	☐	☐		
Follow-up Former Students: reporting on former student success and lack thereof				
Graduates	☐	☐		
Promoted students	☐	☐		
Dropouts	☐	☐		
Teachers and parents	☐	☐		
Universities and employers	☐	☐		
Student Data				
Enrollment/class size	☐	☐		

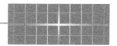

CHECKLIST OF CURRENTLY AVAILABLE AND COLLECTED DATA

Data Source	Currently in School Data	Needs to be collected	Responsibility Who?	When?
Attendance/tardies	☐	☐		
Retention rates	☐	☐		
Discrimination/harassment incident reports	☐	☐		
Discipline referrals/suspensions/expulsions	☐	☐		
Dropout rates/graduation rates (high schools)	☐	☐		
Case facilitation	☐	☐		
Achievement and failure patterns across grade levels	☐	☐		
Standardized test scores, including percentage of students at low, intermediate, and high performance levels in reading and math (grades 4, 8, and 11), plus science and social studies (grades 8 and 11)	☐	☐		
Other school-based assessments	☐	☐		
Stability/mobility of students	☐	☐		
Co-curricular participation	☐	☐		
Disabilities (e.g., IEPs)	☐	☐		
Race/ethnicity	☐	☐		
Gender	☐	☐		
Socio-economic status	☐	☐		

Continued

CHECKLIST OF CURRENTLY AVAILABLE AND COLLECTED DATA

Data Source	Currently in School Data	Needs to be collected	Responsibility Who?	When?
Student Data *(continued)*				
Title I	☐	☐		
Gifted and Talented	☐	☐		
Special education	☐	☐		
Vocational education	☐	☐		
English language learner	☐	☐		
Family structure (including homeless)	☐	☐		
Employment status	☐	☐		
Mobility/transiency	☐	☐		
Length of time in district or school	☐	☐		
Extra-curricular activity participants	☐	☐		
Instructional Data				
Instructional characteristics, including most common instructional techniques used	☐	☐		
Number of sections and FTE teachers per grade level or department	☐	☐		
Student-engaged time	☐	☐		
Staff development opportunities (required/optional)	☐	☐		
School organization/schedule	☐	☐		

CHECKLIST OF CURRENTLY AVAILABLE AND COLLECTED DATA

Data Source	Currently in School Data	Needs to be collected	Responsibility Who?	When?
Support programs	☐	☐		
Important external research and professional literature currently being studied for its relevance to school improvement	☐	☐		
Community Data				
Local, state, federal mandates that impact the school program	☐	☐		
Community programs/facilities	☐	☐		
School/business partnerships	☐	☐		
State/national/international trends and their implications	☐	☐		
Recent community demographic changes (in the school's catchment area)	☐	☐		
Parent and community organizations that encourage and support the school	☐	☐		
Community attitudes toward learning	☐	☐		
Community stakeholder avenues of input to district/schools	☐	☐		

Bernhardt's Four Kinds of Data

Victoria Bernhardt's work (1998) has been very influential on schools in Iowa and in other states. Her basic argument is that schools should gather and use four kinds of data:

- **Student Learning Data**
  (standardized tests, norm- and criterion-referenced tests, teacher observations, and performance assessments)

- **Demographic Data**
  (such indicators as enrollment, attendance, dropout, ethnicity, gender, program participation, grade level, language proficiency, safe and drug-free schools data)

- **Perceptions Data**
  (perception surveys; stakeholder perspectives; values, beliefs, and attitudes; and observations)

- **School Processes Data**
  (descriptions of special programs, strategies, and processes and their effectiveness in terms of impacting student learning)

As the diagram below (adapted from Bernhardt, 1998) represents, these four kinds of data all need to overlap. Indeed, the advantage of using a Venn diagram is that it enables the reader to understand that the overlapping areas are as significant as the four circles themselves. Take "Demographics" for instance; these data allow the disaggregation of not only enrollment, attendance, and dropout rates in terms of various sub-sets of the school population (such as gender, grade, ethnicity, language proficiency), but also student performance (Student Learning Data), stakeholder views (Perceptions Data), and program participation and success/failure rates (School Processes Data). Using this frame, it becomes possible to take one sub-population of students (e.g., those from low socio-economic backgrounds) and map their results across all the various kinds of data.

Multiple Measures of Data

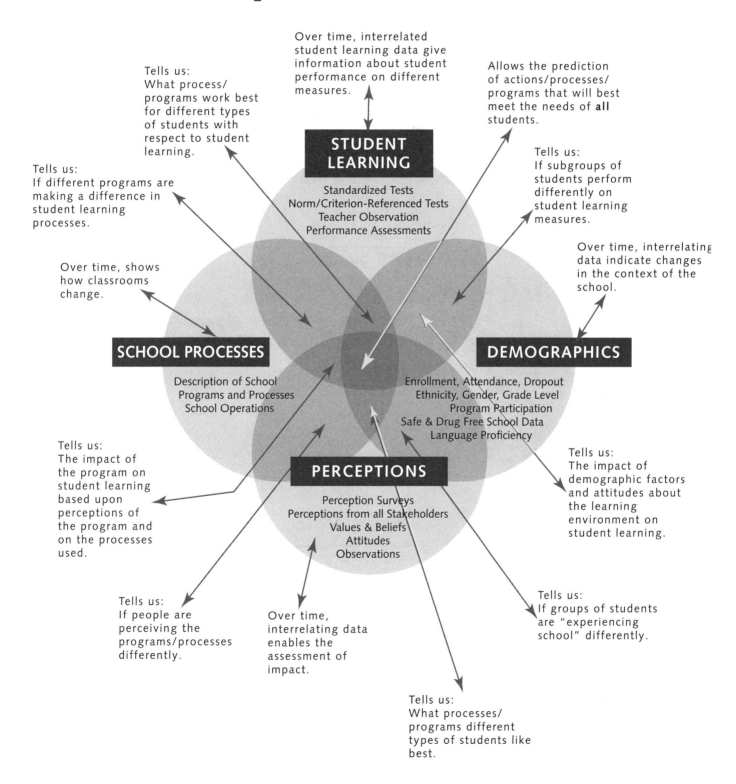

Over time, interrelated student learning data give information about student performance on different measures.

Allows the prediction of actions/processes/programs that will best meet the needs of **all** students.

Tells us: What process/programs work best for different types of students with respect to student learning.

Tells us: If subgroups of students perform differently on student learning measures.

Tells us: If different programs are making a difference in student learning processes.

Over time, interrelating data indicate changes in the context of the school.

Over time, shows how classrooms change.

STUDENT LEARNING

Standardized Tests
Norm/Criterion-Referenced Tests
Teacher Observation
Performance Assessments

SCHOOL PROCESSES

Description of School Programs and Processes
School Operations

DEMOGRAPHICS

Enrollment, Attendance, Dropout
Ethnicity, Gender, Grade Level
Program Participation
Safe & Drug Free School Data
Language Proficiency

PERCEPTIONS

Perception Surveys
Perceptions from all Stakeholders
Values & Beliefs
Attitudes
Observations

Tells us: The impact of the program on student learning based upon perceptions of the program and on the processes used.

Tells us: The impact of demographic factors and attitudes about the learning environment on student learning.

Tells us: If people are perceiving the programs/processes differently.

Over time, interrelating data enables the assessment of impact.

Tells us: If groups of students are "experiencing school" differently.

Tells us: What processes/programs different types of students like best.

Adapted from <u>Education for the Future</u>, Pacific Bell Foundation, San Francisco, 1996, 1997

A Comprehensive Framework for Data Collection

Keeping in mind the advice from the North Central Association's handbook and Bernhardt's four types of data, it becomes possible to construct an interesting data-collection planning matrix. One dimension is Bernhardt's four kinds of data and the other dimension consists of the NCA categories (see below).

NCA Categories	BERNHARDT'S FOUR KINDS OF DATA			
	Student Learning	Demographics	Perceptions	Processes
Unique Local Insights (LI)	LI1	LI2	LI3	LI4
Follow-up of Former Students (FS)	FS5	FS6	FS7	FS8
Existing Data				
Students (ES)	ES9	ES10	ES11	ES12
Instruction (EI)	EI13	EI14	EI15	EI16
Community (EC)	EC17	EC18	EC19	EC20

This planning matrix can be used to map the data collection for a comprehensive school improvement needs assessment. The matrix has 20 cells, starting with Cell 1: LI1 (Local Insights) and ending with Cell 20: EC 20 (Existing Community). For each cell, a "key question" activates the cell. These trigger questions are as follows:

20 Key Questions

LI1: How well do you think our students do in terms of their learning relative to students in other school districts?

LI2: How well do you think sub-populations of our students do in terms of their learning relative to students in other sub-groups?

LI3: What kind of schools do we have in this district?

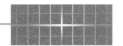
LI4: From your point of view, which programs, classes, and courses are the most effective?

FS5: As a former graduate, what did the schools in this district do to enhance or impede your learning?

FS6: What did the schools do to enhance or impede the learning of various groups of students?

FS7: What are your perceptions of your education in this district?

FS8: Which programs, classes, and courses best equipped you for your life after school?

ES9: What are the current student performance levels and is student learning improving over time?

ES10: What are the current performance levels for various groups of students and are they improving over time?

ES11: How do students view their learning progress?

ES12: Which programs, classes, and courses have the highest achievement and failure rates?

EI13: Which instructional strategies have the most impact on student learning?

EI14: Which instructional strategies work most effectively for which groups of students?

EI15: Which instructional strategies are perceived as being the most effective?

EI16: Which programs, classes, and courses use a range of instructional strategies?

EC17: Which student learnings are most valued by this community?

EC18: Which student groups are represented in this community?

EC19: What are the community perceptions of the local schools?

EC20: According to community views, which programs, classes, and courses could be added to the curriculum and which deleted?

 Reviewing Current Practice
Task 4: Responding to Trigger Questions

Purpose: To consider how the team would go about collecting and using data to answer each of the trigger questions.

Grouping: Work with your Learning Team.

Directions: In your team, discuss—and then describe below—how you would go about answering each of these twenty questions as a comprehensive framework for your needs assessment data collection.

Question	Comments
LI1	
LI2	
LI3	
LI4	
FS5	
FS6	
FS7	
FS8	
ES9	
ES10	
ES11	
ES12	
EI13	
EI14	
EI15	
EI16	
EC17	
EC18	
EC19	
EC20	

Three Things To Keep In Mind

When compiling and learning from a needs assessment, there are three things to keep in mind.

1. Construct and thus reap the benefits of a "triangulation."

2. Make the most of all the data that you have.

3. Replenish the ideas arising from the internal data with the challenges and exhortations that come from a screening of external data.

Triangulation

"Triangulation" is a term borrowed from land surveying; it means getting a more exact bearing on what is going on by looking from three directions or three perspectives. In data gathering, it entails using either three sources of data (to see if they corroborate each other in terms of the emerging story line) or the perspectives of three different sets of respondents (again, to see if their viewpoints are the same). In both cases, if the findings of all three are in agreement, then that tells you something; equally, if they are all in disagreement, then that tells you something else. Where disparities exist, you may want to re-interview—for example—a sample of respondents from each group to find out why their perspectives are so far apart.

Reviewing Current Practice
Task 5: Working with Triangulation

<u>Purpose:</u> To conduct a triangulation exercise.

<u>Directions:</u> On the following pages you will find the "Effective Schools Inventory" (designed by Holly and Sagor, 1989). It is recommended that, as part of a needs assessment, you invite a random sample of parents, teachers, and students to respond to each of the statements and then, in terms of a triangulation, see whether there is a typical "parent view" (and the same for the teachers and students) and whether the three sets of respondents are in agreement or not. Identify which **five** items have the most agreement (positive or negative) across all groups of respondents, which **five** items meet with the most disagreement across all groups, and the reasons why.

EFFECTIVE SCHOOLS INVENTORY

(Holly and Sagor, 1998)

	Strongly Agree	Agree	No Opinion	Disagree	Strongly Disagree
1. Our school maintains high expectations for student behavior.	☐	☐	☐	☐	☐
2. Behavioral expectations are clear at our school.	☐	☐	☐	☐	☐
3. Basic skill achievement in reading, writing, and mathematics is heavily emphasized in our school.	☐	☐	☐	☐	☐
4. Rules are uniformly enforced in our school.	☐	☐	☐	☐	☐
5. Our school is orderly enough for maximum academic concentration.	☐	☐	☐	☐	☐
6. Our school maintains high academic expectations for students.	☐	☐	☐	☐	☐
7. Our faculty really cares about our students.	☐	☐	☐	☐	☐
8. Our faculty works hard to get students to work hard also.	☐	☐	☐	☐	☐
9. Our school gives significant recognition for student behavior.	☐	☐	☐	☐	☐
10. Our school has strong and effective administration leadership.	☐	☐	☐	☐	☐
11. Parents are significantly involved in the programs and activities of our school.	☐	☐	☐	☐	☐
12. Most time spent in classrooms is spent on specific learning tasks.	☐	☐	☐	☐	☐
13. Most curriculum materials are appropriate to student abilities.	☐	☐	☐	☐	☐
14. Students in our school have a significant amount of homework.	☐	☐	☐	☐	☐

EFFECTIVE SCHOOLS INVENTORY

(Holly and Sagor, 1998)

	Strongly Agree	Agree	No Opinion	Disagree	Strongly Disagree
15. Teachers in our school check homework and provide students with feedback.	☐	☐	☐	☐	☐
16. Teachers in our school pay close attention to how students are progressing with their studies.	☐	☐	☐	☐	☐
17. The learning to be accomplished is clearly defined in each course in our school.	☐	☐	☐	☐	☐
18. Our teachers use a great variety of teaching strategies.	☐	☐	☐	☐	☐
19. Teachers in our school employ alternative teaching strategies when students do not seem to be succeeding.	☐	☐	☐	☐	☐
20. Our school provides many opportunities where responsibility is expected from students.	☐	☐	☐	☐	☐
21. A good deal of positive reinforcement and positive feedback is given to students at our school.	☐	☐	☐	☐	☐
22. Teachers expect a great deal of student response in their classrooms.	☐	☐	☐	☐	☐
23. Our school is like a community where students and faculty help each other to share the responsibility for purposeful learning.	☐	☐	☐	☐	☐
24. Our school is a community where people share a common set of values.	☐	☐	☐	☐	☐
25. Teachers in our school enforce the rules even if the student is not in their particular classes.	☐	☐	☐	☐	☐
26. Teachers in our school create materials and activities to meet the learning needs of their students.	☐	☐	☐	☐	☐
27. Our school is structured and organized with learning as the primary goal.	☐	☐	☐	☐	☐
28. Students enjoy going to school at (<u>name of school</u>).	☐	☐	☐	☐	☐

Identify the **five** items having the *most* agreement (positive or negative) across all three groups of respondents:

<u>Agreements</u>   <u>Reasons Why</u>

Item 1:

Item 2:

Item 3:

Item 4:

Item 5:

Identify the **five** items having the *least* agreement (positive or negative) across all three groups of respondents:

<u>Disagreements</u>

Item 1:

Item 2:

Item 3:

Item 4:

Item 5:

Making More of Less Data

As with computers, you get out of a data-collection exercise what you put into it. Put simply, output is determined by input. When it comes to data processing, it pays to have analysis in mind before you start. If, for instance, you are interested in knowing how students from a low socio-economic background respond to certain items on a questionnaire, then "socio-economic background" has to be one of the questions built into the instrument.

In an excellent article on the collection of office referral data, Lo and Cartledge (2001-2) make much the same point. They argue that, in order to allow for meaningful analysis, documentation has to be designed that meets the anticipated needs. Step one, they say, is to design a recording form that contains the following items: student name, date of referral, referring teacher, location of the incident, type of rule violation, brief description of the behavior, and consequence of the action taken. This is probably more than is currently asked of such data. Step two is to transform the referral information into a meaningful form by using some kind of computer spreadsheet program that creates sums, averages, and percentages and presents them in charts, graphs, and tables. Step three involves studying the data: by student (in order to identify occasional and high frequency offenders); by infraction (to see which kinds of problem situations occur most often); and by administrative action (to find out which consequences are applied most often). Summarizing the data is also an important task. Such summaries, say the authors, should include the following:

- total number of students involved

- total number of referrals

- average number of referrals per school day

- average number of referrals per enrolled student

- total number of referred students

- number of frequent offenders

- frequency and type of offenses

- frequency and type of disciplinary action

Lo and Cartledge conclude their article by providing some suggestions for the effective use of data: start analysis early; in terms of statistical analysis, keep it simple; review the data frequently (e.g., on a weekly basis); look for repeat offenders; link the data to interventions (school wide, group, and individual students) to see what is working and what is not; and share the data with teachers and staff.

 Reviewing Current Practice ■ Task 6: Developing
Documentation for Meaningful Analysis

<u>Purpose:</u> To reflect on the benefits of the kind of approach advocated by Lo and
Cartledge.

<u>Grouping:</u> Work with your Learning Team.

<u>Directions:</u> Having read through this advice from Lo and Cartledge, as a team, respond
to the following questions:

1. What are the advantages of this approach and why?

2. What are the obstacles to such an approach and why?

3. How much of this type of approach is done already in your school?

4. What would you like to see added to your approach?

Identifying External Needs

A thorough needs assessment scrutinizes both internal data (for those issues that are unique to the particular school and its setting) and external data (for those needs that are generic and that apply to all schools). Without the former, the needs assessment would have no grounding, no localized bearings. Without the latter, it would have no generalized connections with the needs of schools everywhere. Both kinds of "intelligence" are required for a balanced needs assessment. Each school, therefore, needs to find ways of being continuously linked with the external knowledge base. Whether it is through reading the literature, watching informational videotapes, visiting so-called "lighthouse" sites, attending conferences, or surfing the Internet, the task is the same: to connect with the external world of ideas—to replenish our ideas and re-fuel our imaginations.

 **Reviewing Current Practice**
Task 7: Connecting with External Data

<u>Purpose:</u> To reflect on the availability of external data.

<u>Grouping:</u> Work with your Learning Team.

<u>Directions:</u> Working as a team, describe how your school/school district stays in touch with the external world of ideas.

Analysis of Needs Assessment Data

A crucial element of effective data processing is being able to make sense of the data. While data analysis is the subject of the fourth workbook in this series, *Analyzing and Understanding Data*, a few comments are relevant here. As said previously, a good (i.e., comprehensive) needs assessment casts a wide net in order to catch the most important fish. It is a case of broadening the data base in order to be able to focus on the truly important issues. Emily Calhoun (1990) has listed some "common data analysis questions" as follow:

1. What important points/issues are revealed by these data?

2. What patterns or trends can be identified across the data? Can they be explained?

3. How do data from various sources (e.g., test scores, grades, surveys, interviews, observations, and documentation) compare or contrast?

4. Do any correlations seem important?

5. Are the results different from what you expected?

6. What are the implications for the future?

7. What actions are indicated as being necessary?

During data analysis, then, it is important to be able to trace the *key emerging issues* across various data sources. On the following pages, two mapping charts are provided for accomplishing this major task. The key emerging issues—the priorities for school improvement—are further processed in the third stage of school improvement, Establishing Priorities, which is next discussed in this workbook.

ANALYZING THE PROFILE DATA

Complete the following chart for selected data from your own School Profile.

Data Source (e.g., Discipline Referrals, Surveys, and Test Results)	What are the key findings?	What patterns, connections, or trends show up? How can they be explained?	What are the emerging needs?

DATA ANALYSIS: MAPPING ISSUES FROM THE DATA

Key Emerging Issues	Data Source in Profile				
	Surveys • Parent • Staff • Students	Test Scores	Attendance	Suspensions	Assessment

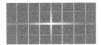 Reviewing Current Practice
Task 8: Using Exemplar Materials

<u>Purpose:</u> To use exemplar materials to discuss how to go about analyzing the data from a comprehensive needs assessment.

<u>Grouping:</u> Work with your Learning Team.

<u>Directions:</u> Discuss in your team, and describe below, how these sample sheets could be used in your situation to begin to identify the main issues and patterns emerging from your needs assessment data. Who could best do this? Who else should be involved and provide input?

What have you learned so far?

What are you continuing to think about?

What are you going to do differently in the future?

Overview

This is the stage of the process when priorities for improvement are identified. It represents another opportunity to involve colleagues in group processing sessions—using appropriate prioritizing techniques. Involvement at this important stage entails the creation of a *shared* agenda for change, which, in turn, is a vital trigger mechanism for establishing staff ownership and commitment (see *Conceptualizing a New Path*). Above all, this is the time to enact the principle of **less is more** by focusing on the agenda items that are indicated as "high priority" in the needs assessment data.

Finding Matching Group Processing Techniques

The task is to select the right technique for the twin purposes of involving colleagues *and* to identify, at the most, three or four "high priority" issues for school-wide development.

There are several techniques that can be used for establishing priorities—the Diamond, the Prioritizing Grid, the Tambourine, Onion Peeling, Pareto Analysis, Cooperative Processing, and Fist of Five and Weighted Voting. They are described and illustrated in the **Group Process Guide** and should be reviewed at this time.

Establishing Priorities for Improvement
Task 1: Reflecting on Group Process Techniques

<u>Purpose:</u> To reflect on the applicability of these various group-processing techniques.

<u>Grouping:</u> Work with your Learning Team.

<u>Directions:</u> As a team, respond to the following questions:

1. How might these specific group-processing techniques for establishing priorities be employed in your school/school district? Which of these techniques do you think would be most effective in your school/school district and why?

2. Describe similar techniques that you have used for prioritizing issues in your school/school district. How successful were these techniques? Why were they successful?

From Prioritizing to Goal Setting

Staff members, working collaboratively and using group processing strategies, can accomplish the following major task of moving from a list of priorities to the identification of school improvement goals. As an organizing framework, the "4 Cs Frame" introduced in the first workbook, *Conceptualizing a New Path*, will be used. The 4 Cs include:

- Challenging Expectations for All Learners

- Curriculum: Process and Content

- Climate

- Collaboration

A diagram of the 4 Cs Frame follows for your review.

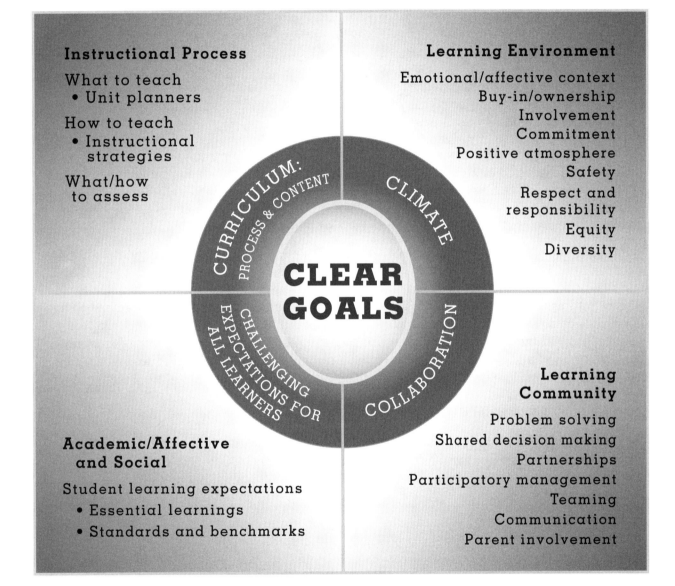

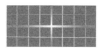 **Establishing Priorities for Improvement**
Task 2: Using the 4 Cs Frame to Identify Goals

<u>Purpose:</u> To use the 4Cs frame as an organizer for moving from priorities to the identification of school improvement goals.

<u>Grouping:</u> Work in small groups (4 to 7 people preferably from a mix of grades/subjects) and as a whole group. A recorder/reporter should be selected for each small group.

<u>Group process strategy:</u> Suggested strategies are discussed within each step. Groups may choose other strategies as they feel are appropriate for their groups and situations. Refer to the **Group Process Guide** as needed.

NOTE: The simpler techniques of Fist of Five or Weighted Voting may also be used, either independently or along with other group process strategies suggested below.

<u>Directions:</u> For this task, you will be moving through the following four steps to reach the task objective of identifying four school improvement goal statements.

<u>Step One: Listing Priority Issues</u>

Each small group is to create a list of the priority issues that emerge from the collected data. A suggested approach is to have team members individually jot down three to five priorities and then share these using a group processing strategy such as the Go Round or the Cooperative Processing strategy of In-Turn Response. To come to consensus on the group list, the Tambourine technique or the Cooperative Processing Decision/Voting Component would be appropriate.

<u>Step Two: Sorting Issues Using the 4 Cs Frame</u>

In the same teams and using the 4 Cs frame shown below, sort the issues into the four areas: Challenging Expectations, Curriculum: Process and Content, Climate, and Collaboration.

Curriculum: Process and Content

Climate

Challenging Expectations

Collaboration

Step Three: Choosing Provisional Goals

Each small group chooses a provisional goal for each of the four areas and reports out to the whole group. For this activity, the Onion Peeling strategy would be appropriate.

Step Four: Finalizing the Goal Statements

The whole staff comes to consensus on a composite version of the four goals. Small work groups are assigned the task of finalizing the wording of the goal statement for one of the four goals using the "Writing a Goal Statement" box that follows.

WRITING A GOAL STATEMENT

Example:

Our goal is to [1]improve the [2]level of student [3]engagement with [4]language/career development.

1	2	3
DEVELOP	QUALITY	PERFORMANCE
INCREASE	AMOUNT	ACHIEVEMENT
ENHANCE	DEGREE	ACCOMPLISHMENT
IMPROVE	LEVEL	ENGAGEMENT
WIDEN	EXTENT	ATTITUDES
		LEARNING

4
CONTEXT/AREA OF
SCHOOL IMPROVEMENT

Matrix Planning

As part of the school improvement process, it is often important to show the relationship between building goals and district goals. Given the fact that they are data driven, there may not be an exact fit between the two sets of goals. Matrix planning, however, allows for "docking" between the goals. It enables school people to see that their internal goals (in which they have ownership and to which they have commitment) are not being dictated by external goals but are in correspondence with them. Looking across the district as an interlocking system, matrix planning also shows the **contributions** that a particular school is making to the collective effort.

The technique is simple to operate. One axis of the matrix consists of the building's data-based needs (again, the 4 Cs can be used as a frame for reference) and the other axis is made up of the district goals. The school goals can then be inserted on the inside of the matrix and plotted across from each dimension (see the example below).

BUILDING NEEDS	Continuous Improvement	Personalized Learning	Integration	Optimum Use of Human Resources	Diversity
All Students not Learning at Highest Level (Challenging Expectations)	Goal 1: to increase student achievement through effective instructional strategies.	Goal 2: to increase opportunities for students to work in smaller groups and one-on-one with teachers.			
Curriculum Not Meeting Needs of Students (Curriculum: Process and Content)			Goal 3: to increase student achievement through curriculum modification.		
Few Parents Involved in the Education of Their Child (Collaboration)				Goal 4: to increase parent involvement through partnerships with parents and community.	
Lack of Student Responsibility and Respect for Others (Climate)					Goal 5: to implement a social skills program which will develop caring, responsible citizens.

DISTRICT GOALS

Establishing Priorities for Improvement
Task 3: Using Matrix Planning

<u>Purpose:</u> To use matrix planning in a local setting.

<u>Grouping:</u> Work with your Learning Team.

<u>Directions:</u> This is your opportunity to use matrix planning for your district. On the chart below, plot the goal "contributions" of the elementary, middle, and high schools and how they correspond with the district goals.

Contributions	K-12 District Goal 1: _____	K-12 District Goal 2: _____	K-12 District Goal 3: _____	K-12 District Goal 4: _____
Elementary				
Middle				
High				

What have you learned so far?

What are you continuing to think about?

What are you going to do differently in the future?

Notes

Stage 4

Action Planning

Overview

Action Planning is the crux of the school improvement process. When the author (1990) designed his "1, 4, 5, 2, 3" approach to action planning, he had two considerations very much in mind. First, he had been asked by a group of teachers to help them in their change efforts. "Why is it," they asked, "that school improvement always feels like punching into a cloud? Why can't it be clearer?" Second, he had come across the following advice:

> In schools, clear and shared goals provide unity, help channel and target resources within the school program, can foster collaboration and establish criteria for school success that permit assessment of progress...this takes the form of a clear vision of what the school should be, which is translated into concrete objectives and communicated to the staff in such a way as to influence what they do in their professional roles...written school improvement plans can be a road map for creating and realizing a shared vision of what the school should be (Patterson et al., 1986).

Three particular points from this quotation helped him understand what had to be done to clear up some of the "cloudiness" of school improvement.

- Clear and shared goals not only create resource-driven unity and focus, but also, and crucially, lead to the generation of more specific success criteria—the specific elements of the goals.

- These success criteria can be used for two vital purposes. First, because they spring from the goals that, in turn, should be aligned with the guiding vision, the success criteria link the vision with the everyday world of classroom practice— they guide teachers in the fulfillment of their professional roles. Second, they can also be used to assess the progress over time of the school improvement goals; they are the specific elements of the goals that have to be achieved if the goals are to be accomplished. It is the specificity of success criteria that militates against the "cloudiness" of school improvement.

- A school improvement action plan is a detailed road map for how to go about making the desired changes. It creates certainty and specificity (rather than "cloudiness"), however flexibly it is implemented.

A Taxonomy of School Improvement

At the school level:

- **Concerns** are intuitive concerns.

- **Needs** are concerns grounded and substantiated in data.

- **Goals** are statements of improvement-related intentions in the areas of need.

- **Success Criteria** are the essential elements that have to be achieved if the goals are to be accomplished.

- **Implementation Strategies** are the change vehicles used to reach our goals and success criteria.

- **Assessments** are the techniques that will be used to show that the success criteria have indeed been achieved.

What is clear in this taxonomy is the degree of alignment required in a solid action plan. Success criteria, implementation strategies, and assessments should all be aligned with the goals, which in turn, should be aligned with the original guiding vision.

Action Planning
Task 1: Reflecting on the Role of Success Criteria

Purpose: To reflect on the role played by success criteria in the participants' local school improvement efforts.

Grouping: Work with your Learning Team.

Group process strategy: This would be a good opportunity to try a brainstorming strategy such as the Round-Robin Brainstorm (refer to the **Group Process Guide**).

Directions: In your team, discuss and answer the following questions using a brainstorming strategy.

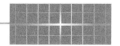

1. Do you have the equivalent of success criteria in your school improvement plan? If so, list them and explain how they are used. If not, how could they be inserted?

2. Do you have the degree of alignment in your school improvement plan suggested above? If the answer is "yes," provide examples; if "no," discuss how to go about improving and strengthening the alignment in your plan.

Applying the "1, 4, 5, 2, 3" Planning Process

Having realized the pivotal importance of success criteria, the author designed the "1, 4, 5, 2, 3" planner to honor their centrality in the action planning process. The planning process is called "1, 4, 5, 2, 3" because this title reflects the sequence of steps used to fill in the planning sheet that follows. **Column 1** of the sheet is the *Goal Statement*. Indeed, the planner is for *one goal only*. For four goals, for example, four planning sheets would be required. According to this design, the planners then go straight to **Column 4** and divide the goal into its specific, constituent parts in order to identify the *Success Criteria/Specific Outcomes*. While working with success criteria, it makes sense to then go to **Column 5** identified as *Data Collection Methods*, and list the ways that data will be collected to chart progress over time and provide evidence that the success criteria have been achieved. Next, the planning sequence involves the completion of **Column 2** (*Implementation Strategies*) and **Column 3** (*Support Needs*).

Beginning with the End in Mind

By working on **Columns 4** and **5** before **Columns 2** and **3**, participants are able to follow Covey's (1989) advice by "beginning with the end in mind." In so doing, the monitoring and evaluation of school improvement efforts are brought up front (as opposed to them being an after-thought, which was so often the case previously) and the concept of data-driven school improvement is actualized. The participants, from the outset, know what is required of them, what success will need to look like, and what data collection methods will be used to track their progress.

ACTION PLANNING SHEET

1	2
Goal Statement	**Implementation Strategies**

	Timeline	Strategies	Person(s) Responsible

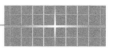

3	4	5
Support Needs	**Success Criteria/ Specific Outcomes**	**Data Collection Methods**
<u>Needs</u> <u>Costs</u>	"Success will have been achieved when…"	Baseline: Up close: Trend line:

The '1,4,5,2,3' approach creates the need for two levels of monitoring and evaluation. Level one has already been mentioned—it involves mapping progress toward the success criteria over time. Success criteria should be framed in terms of student learning and are very similar to **student learning results** or **student learning outcomes** (see Schmoker, 1996). Level two involves scrutiny of the teachers' implementation efforts. Are the implementation strategies being used in textbook style; are they being used effectively? Are they being used in ways that are likely to lead to the accomplishment of the success criteria?

Recently, Champion (2002) has taken Kirkpatrick's 4-level model (reaction, learning, use, and results) and applied it to staff development activities—which are often the vital link between action planning and implementation. The fourth level focuses on student learning results and the other three levels (see below) refer to the stages of teacher implementation.

Level One: Data to Evaluate Reaction/Awareness

Key question: *How did participants respond to the training?*

- immediate feedback; record of comments
- continuing voluntary participation
- exit interviews, surveys
- requests for materials
- observations of participants' behavior
- results of follow-up inquiries

Level Two: Data to Evaluate Trainee Learning

Key question: *Do the participants know how to apply the new learning?*

- scores on pre- and post-assessments
- quality of learning products
- demonstration of understanding/skills on performance tasks
- workplace observations to determine degree of application

- reports from principals

- completed classroom assignments

- content analysis of logs and journals

- performance of individuals during training
  exercises

Level Three: Data to Evaluate Full Implementation of the New Learning

Key question: *Are the ideas gained in the training being fully implemented?*

- observations

- training homework/assignments/classroom
  application projects

- reports from principals

- content analysis of logs and journals

- participants' self-reported descriptions

- student work

- reports from students and their parents

Level Four: Data to Evaluate Results

Key question: *What is the impact on student learning results?*

- school records of student progress

- student test scores

- student work/portfolios

- reports from students and their parents

- artifacts (e.g., meeting minutes, lesson and
  unit plans)

Emily Calhoun's (1999) advice to schools in terms of putting all available resources behind one important goal serves to underline the importance of the "1,4,5,2,3" approach. She makes four points of great relevance here.

- The focus on one powerful goal limits the amount of student learning data to collect, the amount of data to collect about what is currently happening in curriculum and instruction throughout the school, the extensiveness of the study of the external knowledge base, and the application of high quality staff development.

- Having the goal helps us focus; then we push it through to the things that everyone must be doing to bring it into reality. By "seeing through and beyond the goal" (a crucial concept), all the required changes and supports can be planned as follows:

  - The faculty members need to look through the learning goal to the student performances they want to see and what successful goal attainment would look like in terms of student learning.

  - Then, they need to determine what teacher behaviors in curriculum, instruction, and assessment are necessary to promote those student behaviors.

  - This extends to what the principal and central office staff should be doing.

- Teachers must look beyond the data that are readily available, such as standardized test scores and grades, into the specific student performances (success criteria) they're trying to develop. In reading comprehension, for example:

  - Can students identify the main idea of a passage?

  - Can they explain how they determined the main idea?

  - Can they use multiple sources of information in forming major ideas about a topic? Can students identify the author's purpose?

- Teachers must reach out to the external knowledge base to interact with the ideas of others. Study time should be used to help faculty members to select classroom strategies that are likely to yield increases in student achievement and learn how to use them at a high level of skill.

Schmoker (1996) in *Results: the Key to Continuous Improvement* emphasizes the pivotal importance of a goal-based approach. He begins by quoting McGonagill (1992):

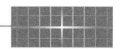

> The annual goal statements that emerge from school improvement efforts are rarely linked to student achievement, and they seldom challenge the basic elements of practice.

Consequently, Schmoker calls for goals that

■ are clear and measurable

■ lead to results that, in turn, are a "thoughtfully established, desired end-product"

■ are accompanied by "good faith efforts to collectively and regularly monitor and adjust actions"

■ are "clear, elevating" and give meaning to teamwork (Teams, he says, enjoy pursuing doable goals that they value.)

■ have sub-goals that are the responsibility of sub-units (action teams)

■ are specific ("I believe," he says, "that specific goals are the most vital ingredient of purpose." Goals that are too general provide what he calls false clarity and, "when specific goals do not exist, one-shot staff development or high sounding programs often fill the void.")

■ promote the improvement of student learning ("Without explicit learning goals," he says, "we are simply not set up and organized for improvement, for results." The success of school improvement efforts should not be judged by whether innovations have been implemented but by whether the students have learned.)

■ are objectives as opposed to innovations (See his examples on the next page.)

Goals: The Missing Piece in Reform *(Results: the Key to Continuous Improvement,* Schmoker, 1996)

Goals and Subgoals

Goal: Students will write well.

Subgoals:

- Write effective introductions.
- Provide supporting details.

Goal: Students will excel in math.

Subgoals:

- Describe and understand the steps to solve problems.
- Compute more accurately.
- Apply mathematical knowledge to practical situations.

Goal: Students will excel in science.

Subgoals:

- Demonstrate mastery of scientific knowledge.
- Conduct a rigorous experiment.
- Make a presentation proposing a solution to a scientific or technological problem.

Innovations Compared to Objectives

Innovation	Objective
Technology	Students will learn how to use various forms of technology to improve their performance.
Cooperative Learning	Students will learn how to operate in groups, and their achievement and attitudes will reflect the skills learned.
Whole-Language Instruction	Students will acquire a more positive attitude toward reading, read with more comprehension, and write more creatively and analytically.
Interdisciplinary Instruction	Students will be better able to solve problems by drawing from the various disciplines.

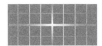 Action Planning
Task 2: Understanding the Action Planning Process

Purpose: To work through the steps of the action planning process for one particular school improvement goal.

Grouping: It is highly recommended that, as a team, you work through the action planning activities contained in Task 2 for one of your *current school improvement goals*. It will make this work more meaningful to have a real-life application that is important to your team. If this is not possible or appropriate for your situation, this work may take the form of a training simulation.

Directions: This task is sub-divided into twelve Action Planning Activities. The directions for each activity are explained as you move through the action planning process. Through these twelve steps, you are completing the five columns on the Action Planning Sheet in the order of "1, 4, 5, 2, 3" as previously explained. Unless otherwise stated, you will work with your Learning Team on each activity.

Task 2: Understanding the Action Planning Process

Activity 1—Writing a Goal Statement

Purpose: To produce a well-written goal statement.

Writing a Goal Statement (Column 1)

Using the discussion from the previous section of this workbook, you are to record below one major goal statement that has four components: an active verb, the "qualifier" (the degree or amount of intended success), the intended impact on students and their learning, and the area of school improvement concerned.

Goal Statement:

Task 2: Understanding the Action Planning Process

Activity 2—Evaluating the Goal Statement

<u>Purpose:</u> To evaluate the quality of the goal statement.

Now ask these review questions of your goal statement:

- Is it well constructed?

- Is it focused enough but not too specific? (Remember that increased specificity comes in Column 4.)

- Is it clearly stated?

- Is it sufficiently needs-based data-driven?

- Does it span various concerns and issues?

- Is its importance understood and shared by the staff-at-large?

- Is it aligned with the school's vision?

- Is it grounded in both internal and external data?

Remember:

> **It is important not to confuse goals with implementation strategies.**
>
> <u>YES</u>
>
> Goal: to improve reading comprehension
>
> <u>NO</u>
>
> Goal: to introduce Guided Reading

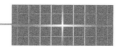

Do your answers to any of the review questions make you want to revise your goal statement? If so, insert the revisions below.

Revised Goal Statement:

For Column 1: Enter your shared and agreed upon single goal statement on the blank Action Planning Sheet that follows on the next page.

ACTION PLANNING SHEET		
1	**2**	
Goal Statement	**Implementation Strategies**	
	Timeline	Strategies	Person(s) Responsible

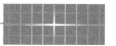

3	4	5
Support Needs	**Success Criteria/ Specific Outcomes**	**Data Collection Methods**
<u>Needs</u> <u>Costs</u>	"Success will have been achieved when…"	Baseline: Up close: Trend line:

Task 2: Understanding the Action Planning Process

Activity 3—Generating Success Criteria/Specific Outcomes

<u>Purpose:</u> To generate Success Criteria/Specific Outcomes (Column Four).

<u>Group process strategy:</u> Various techniques can be used to generate success criteria. Some examples are as follows:

Onion Peeling

This technique is described in the **Group Process Guide**. This time it can be used to achieve depth and specificity by dividing the goal in the top circle into its constituent elements and then selecting one of these constituent elements as high priority and moving it to the middle of the lower circle and separating it in terms of even more specific detail.

Completing the Unfinished Sentence

Success criteria can be generated by repeatedly completing the unfinished sentence. For example: "Success will have been achieved, when…"

Trigger Questions

Answering trigger questions, such as the following, can generate success criteria:

- Why is this goal important for us?

- What are we trying to achieve?

- In what ways does this goal help us realize our vision?

- What will constitute success?

- What should it look like?

- How will we know when we've gotten there?

- What will we show as evidence of our success?

Brainstorming

In answer to the question, "Why did we choose this goal?" brainstorm twenty *reasons* why this goal was chosen. Twenty seems to be the magic number. The responses that are elicited early in the process are usually the more obvious ones; the responses that are more difficult to unearth come later in the process and are often the more important ones. In order to become success criteria, the language used in the responses often has to be slightly amended. For instance, if the goal is focused on the need for improved student behavior school wide and one of the reasons cited is, "too much fighting," then the success criterion becomes: a reduction in the number of recorded fights in the school.

<u>Directions:</u> As a team, use the Round-Robin brainstorming technique (see the **Group Process Guide**) to generate success criteria for your selected goal. Brainstorm *twenty* reasons why you chose this particular goal (record the reason in the left-hand column of the following chart) and then change the language slightly to translate the reasons into success criteria (record in the right-hand column).

Twenty Reasons	Re-worded Success Criteria

In order to further articulate your goal, review your list of Success Criteria pertaining to the goal recorded in Column 1. These criteria should be detailed, concrete, specific, and above all, essential to student learning.

Your list can take the form of multiple responses to the unfinished sentence: "*Success will have been achieved when...*"

Remember that success criteria are

- student learning centered

- results orientated

- measurable, if at all possible

Example

Goal: Increase student proficiency levels in reading and language arts.

Success Criteria: The number of *students reading*[1] *at or above grade level*[2] will *increase by 5%*[3] during the current school year.

[1] Student learning centered
[2] Results orientated
[3] Measurable (with a time specified)

Task 2: Understanding the Action Planning Process

Activity 4—Evaluating the Success Criteria

Purpose: To evaluate the quality of the success criteria.

Now ask these review questions of your success criteria:

- Are they detailed, concrete, specific, demonstrable, and measurable?

- Are they focused on student learning results?

- Are they quantifiable and time-bound? For example, "the number of students reading at or above grade level will increase by 5% during the current school year."

- Are they connected to the district's expectations for learning (such as Essential Learnings, exit level and/or grade level performance standards)?

- Are they capable of acting as sign posts (Are we going in the right direction?), mile posts (Are we making headway? How far are we getting?) and destination markers/outcome indicators (Have we gotten there?)

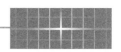
Success criteria should demonstrate the achievement of the goal, not the performance of the implementation strategy.

<u>YES</u>

Success Criteria: 70% of the students will achieve at the proficiency level or above on the state-mandated reading comprehension subtest.

<u>NO</u>

Success Criteria: 70% of teachers will introduce Guided Reading in their classrooms.

For Column 4: Success Criteria/Specific Outcomes

After using the review questions and the advice provided above, make any necessary amendments and record your final list of Success Criteria in **Column 4** of the Action Planning Sheet.

Task 2: Understanding the Action Planning Process

Activity 5A—Identifying Data Collection Methods (Column 5)

<u>Purpose:</u> To work across from each of the success criteria and identify appropriate methods for collecting baseline data, up-close data, and trend-line data in order to monitor and evaluate the degree of impact of each success criterion/exit outcome.

Baseline data provide

- information concerning the goal/success criterion—prior to improvement efforts being initiated

- the current status in the area in question

- the starting line against which all progress in this area can be measured

- quantifiable evidence (e.g., 60% of parents and 25% of teachers think class cutting is a problem)

Up-close data

- are gathered frequently (e.g., weekly or monthly)

- involve the close monitoring of the action

- are collected *during* implementation

- capture the responses and feelings of different groups of participants and, as such, are more impressionistic, more anecdotal, more qualitative

- can be used as immediate feedback, thus allowing mid-course corrections and adjustments to be made

Trend-line data

- are baseline data revisited at regular (e.g., annual) intervals over time

- show growth relative to the original baseline

- provide evidence of goal attainment

Up-close data are a comparative newcomer to school improvement activities. Emerging from the practice of classroom action research, Calhoun (1999) describes them as "data as close to the student performance as possible" and suggests that they are collected on a weekly, bi-weekly, or monthly basis.

<u>Techniques for Gathering Up-Close Data</u>

- Reflective diaries, logs, and journals

- Students' work in portfolios

- Informal quizzes, end-of-chapter tests

- Observations

- Scored rubrics

- Short surveys

- Reading probes

- Walk-about studies

- Photographs/videotapes

- Interviews/informal conversations

- Work samples from selected students collaboratively screened and scored by teacher team members

Task 2: Understanding the Action Planning Process

Activity 5B—Selecting Data Collection Methods

Purpose: To determine which data collection methods to use for tracking progress over time.

Working as a team and using the chart below as a worksheet, map the data collection methods to be used for each of the success criteria listed on your Action Planning Sheet. It should be noted that the same methods might suffice for several success criteria.

Success Criteria/ Specific Outcomes	DATA COLLECTION METHODS		
	Baseline Data	Up-close Data	Trend-line Data

121

Task 2: Understanding the Action Planning Process

Activity 6—Evaluating Data Collection Methods

Purpose: To evaluate the quality of the selected data collection methods.

Now ask these review questions of your data collection plans:

- Have baseline, up-close, and trend-line data collection methods been identified for each success criterion?

- Have the same data collection methods been selected for more than one success criterion?

- Even so, is there enough variety across the methods chosen?

- Are the selected methods appropriate for the tasks at hand?

- Is there a balance between quantitative and qualitative data collection methods?

- Will the selected data collection methods enable you to formatively monitor your progress over time?

- Will the selected data collection methods enable you to summatively evaluate your progress and check for goal attainment?

Looking back at your data map, is it sufficient or have these questions triggered thoughts about required amendments? What amendments would you like to make?

For Column 5: Data Collection Methods

When you have finalized the data collection methods, transfer this information to **Column 5** of your Action Planning Sheet.

Moving to Column 2: Implementation Strategies

Now is the time to consider the actions to be taken in order to achieve success. Looking back at Column 4, the questions to ask are as follows: "If all those things have to be accomplished, what would get us there?" and "In which order?" It's a case of selecting those strategies that are most likely to lead to success in the particular goal area and then designing a sequence of action steps for the introduction and implementation of these strategies. Implicit in the construction of Column 2 are the following: a sequence of events and activities, timelines, action steps, and staff tasks and responsibilities.

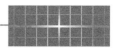

Remember:

> Implementation strategies are the interventions, the vehicles chosen to work on in order to achieve the goal/success criteria.
>
> <u>YES</u>
>
> Guided Reading
>
> <u>NO</u>
>
> 70% of students will increase their proficiency on the state-mandated reading comprehension subtest.

Task 2: Understanding the Action Planning Process

Activity 7—The Implementation Plan

<u>Purpose:</u> To detail the elements of an implementation plan.

This is your opportunity, using the following chart, to turn to the vital question of implementation—in terms of a timeline, steps/tasks/strategies, and those persons responsible. Record your prioritized list of action steps/implementation strategies, remembering to be **S.M.A.R.T.** by identifying **S**pecific tasks, which are **M**easurable (i.e., demonstrably accomplished), **A**chievable, **R**ealistic, and **T**ime-bound.

**WHAT TO DO? WHEN TO DO THEM?
HOW TO DO THEM/WHO'S RESPONSIBLE?**

IMPLEMENTATION PLAN		
Timeline	**Implementation Strategies** (Steps/Tasks/Strategies)	**Person(s) Responsible**

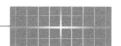

Task 2: Understanding the Action Planning Process

Activity 8—Evaluating the Implementation Plan

<u>Purpose:</u> To evaluate the quality of the implementation plan.

Now ask these review questions of your implementation plan:

- Are the selected implementation strategies likely to significantly impact student learning? How will you know?

- Are the selected implementation strategies likely to lead to the achievement of the desired learning outcomes? Put simply, will they deliver the goods? How will you know?

- Were the strategies selected as a result of an extensive review of the external knowledge base? Do they have a proven track record?

- Do we intend to amend or adjust the use of our strategies during implementation? Are we organized to receive feedback during the implementation process so we can make the necessary "in-flight" adjustments?

- Are the timelines challenging yet achievable?

- Are personal responsibilities clear and reasonable? Is the implementation load sufficiently shared?

- Is the sequence of steps and tasks well designed?

For Column 2: Implementation Strategies

Once again, having responded to these review questions, review your Implementation Plan and make necessary adjustments. When you have revised your plan to your group's satisfaction, transfer this information to **Column 2** of the Action Planning Sheet.

Moving to Column 3: Providing for Support Needs

Column 3 entails the mobilization of all the supports that will help staff members be successful in their implementation efforts. Staff training and professional development opportunities top the list. As is acknowledged in the "less is more" approach, major change efforts only succeed when they are packaged for success. Support packages have to include planning time (for arranging the classroom application of the required changes) as well as ongoing training opportunities, resource provisions (including the allocation of time for collaborative dialogue), teamwork, and the reflective monitoring of change efforts. This is also the time to apply the messages from adult learning theory and provide opportunities for staff learning that incorporate the elements of effective staff development identified by Joyce and Showers (1982). Coaching is key.

This is why time has to be set aside for peer observation, peer coaching, and reflective conversations between implementing teachers. Without this level of intensity it may well prove impossible to survive the early days of implementation—referred to by Michael Fullan as the "implementation dip"—when teachers are feeling de-skilled, over-challenged, and lacking in confidence. What is required is "scaffolding" that encourages and supports early implementation efforts and discourages those involved from taking the easy option and returning to their former practice.

Task 2: Understanding the Action Planning Process

Activity 9—The Implementation Dip

<u>Purpose:</u> To reflect on the reasons for the implementation dip.

In your team, discuss the reasons why so many change efforts "fall at the first fence" and then list the reasons below.

Task 2: Understanding the Action Planning Process

Activity 10—A Support Package for Implementation Efforts

<u>Purpose:</u> To construct a support package for your implementation efforts.

Having reflected on why the change process often breaks down at this point, this is your opportunity to marshal all the necessary supports that will enable your implementation efforts to be successful. With your team, identify and prioritize both your support needs (resources, including time, software and hardware, and people, plus training and professional development needs) and their likely costs using the chart below. How much can you afford to do with the available resources? What is your rationale for each listed support?

Support Needs	Likely Costs

Task 2: Understanding the Action Planning Process

Activity 11—Evaluating the Support Package

<u>Purpose:</u> To evaluate the quality of the support package.

Now ask these review questions of your support plans:

- Have you organized an intensive support package?

- Will it be powerful enough to get colleagues across the implementation dip?

- Have you identified the funding streams that will pay for the support package?

- Do your plans include **time** for staff members to work together and support each other in their implementation efforts?

For Column 3: Support Needs

Again, in the light of these questions, review your plans and make any necessary adjustments. Are any changes required? After you have made any needed adjustments, transfer this information to **Column 3** of your Action Planning sheet.

The following flowchart provides an example of an Action Planning Sheet where the "1, 4, 5, 2, 3" Planning Process has been applied.

THE 1,4,5,2,3 PLANNING PROCESS

COLUMN 1

GOAL STATEMENT

To explore ways of serving students at risk for ...

COLUMN 2

IMPLEMENTATION STRATEGIES

Introduce cross-age tutoring and review teaching styles generally

Chart monthly attendance and act on findings

Initiate new approaches to self-assessment (in order to capture achievement and, therefore, increase self-esteem). Introduce "student-as-worker" strategies

COLUMN 3

SUPPORT NEEDS

Training for staff and students on cross-age tutoring

Training for staff and students on the importance and impact of heightening self-esteem and strategies for achieving it

COLUMN 4

SUCCESS CRITERIA/ SPECIFIC OUTCOMES

Improvements in social behavior, e.g., less fighting, more cooperation in the classroom

Better attendance

Improvements in the students' self-concept/self-esteem

Improvements in academic accomplishments, e.g., grades

COLUMN 5

DATA COLLECTION METHODS

Keep a count of discipline notices

Observation—fewer cases of confrontation in the classroom; more cases of cooperation between students and between students and teachers

Check attendance records

Standardized test scores, plus more authentic assessment

Interview students and parents

129

Common Errors in the Action Planning Process

Because of the pivotal nature of action planning, it is important to avoid some of the common errors made in the process.

■ There is a tendency to plan as it has always been done and, once the goal has been selected, to go straight to Column 2 (Implementation Strategies). This approach completely loses the power of generating success criteria and, therefore, knowing where you're going before you begin. Success criteria can act as magnets, pulling you into the future.

■ Too often, goals and strategies are confused. "To implement Guided Reading" is a *strategy*, not a goal (which, in this instance, is to improve reading proficiency). Schmoker (1996) mentions this same issue and differentiates between "objectives" (goals) and "innovations" (implementation strategies).

■ Success criteria have to be specific, measurable, and geared to student learning results. If any of these ingredients are missing, the power of success criteria is compromised.

■ The support issue is vital. If support plans are omitted or are flimsy at best, then implementation efforts are doomed from the outset.

■ Action plans need to be clearly stated and aligned across the columns. The success criteria need to support the goal, the implementation strategies should enable the participants to achieve the success criteria, and the support package (support needs) should render implementation viable and effective. Too many plans become cluttered with unnecessary detail and are misaligned. In Dubuque Schools, to ease the problem of excess detail, a section has been created in the school improvement plan for "Continuing Initiatives" (commonly referred to as the "parking lot")—all those activities that have been introduced, implemented, and are now in need of ongoing maintenance. These initiatives are still important to the school involved, but don't require the same intensity of attention and don't need to be in the current **implementation** plans.

■ Action planning is a great opportunity for getting everyone involved. This is why all faculty members should be encouraged to join the action team of their choice. This level of expectation, however, is not always present.

Task 2: Understanding the Action Planning Process

Activity 12—Planning Errors

<u>Purpose:</u> To discuss the errors that can undermine the potential power of action planning.

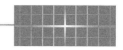

In your team, discuss these planning errors—and others—in terms of your own experiences and answer these two questions:

1. Which planning errors have been made in your context? Why do you think they were made and how could they have been avoided?

2. How can you go about doing things differently? In what ways will this be important?

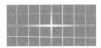

Action Planning
Task 3: Applying New Knowledge

<u>Purpose:</u> To use exemplar materials to apply new knowledge about action planning.

<u>Grouping:</u> Work in pairs and then meet with your Learning Team to share responses.

<u>Directions:</u> There are three parts to this task. This is a major opportunity to work with your new knowledge and to apply the following "Quality Criteria for Implementation Strategies" to several examples. In Part 1, you use the Quality Criteria to rate Implementation Strategies for three sample action plans. In Part 2, you rate the selection of Implementation Strategies on your own completed Action Planning Sheet using the same Quality Criteria. And in Part 3, you complete Column 5 (Data Collection Methods) and Column 2 (Implementation Strategies) for three sample action plans.

Quality Criteria for Implementation Strategies

Implementation Strategies are

- relevant and appropriate

- drawn from the external data base

- well-matched to identified internal needs

- customized for local use

- well-suited to flexible diagnostic application

- applicable to sustained systematic implementation

- likely to have staff support and commitment

Part 1

a. Read Sample Action Planning Sheets A, B, and C that follow.

b. Using the quality criteria listed above, rate the selection of Implementation Strategies (Column 2) in the three samples using the following chart and a scale of 1-5, where 1 = Minimally; 3 = To a large extent; 5 = Absolutely.

Quality Criteria	Sample:		
	A	B	C
Relevance and appropriateness			
Drawn from the external data base			
Well-matched to identified internal needs			
Customized for local use			
Well-suited to flexible diagnostic application			
Applicable to sustained, systematic implementation			
Likely to have staff support and commitment			

Sample A:

DISTRICT GOAL: IMPROVE STUDENT ACHIEVEMENT PK-12				
Goal Statement What is/are our school's goal area(s) to reach the district-wide goal?	**Implementation Strategies** What are our action steps we will take to reach our school's goal?	**Success Criteria/ Specific Outcomes** What measurable results do we expect for students?	**Data Collection Methods** How will we collect data to measure our progress towards the goal?	
			Baseline/Trend-line Data	Up-close Data
1.1 Mesh all reading initiatives and best teaching practices to improve student achievement.	1.1.1 Implement "Every Child Reads" strategies and the EL Literacy Platform through the use of non-fiction texts in expeditions, integrating reading across all curricular areas.	1.1.1 100% of all the students will have more contact with non-fiction texts.	1.1.1 #books currently in LRC and classrooms earmarked for expeditions, science, social studies.	1.1.1 Lesson plans and peer coaching log.
	1.1.2 Staff will conduct tuning protocols for expedition critique and collaboration assessment conferences for examining student work together.	1.1.2 For 85% or more of the students, quality of work will improve over a series of drafts.	1.1.2 Baseline will be established 2003-04 by assessing first and final copies of student's work through a scored common rubric.	1.1.2 Classroom assessment (rubric).
1.2 Improve achievement by focusing on the development of interventions to address students whose academic and behavior needs are not meeting expected standards.	1.2.1 Collaborate between general education staff, special education staff, counselor, nurse, principal and AEA staff to use the Problem Solving Model to identify and address student needs.	1.2.1 After the test packet is developed, 100% of students entering during the school year will be assessed in reading, writing, and math within a month of their arrival. 100% of general education teachers will attend Problem Solving meetings.	1.2.1 Data collected from new student packet will be shared with classroom teacher. Data collected on student stage forms and through minutes of the Problem Solving Team.	1.2.1 Forms determined by team.
1.b.1 Increase student proficiency levels in math.	1.b.1.1 Differentiate content, process, and product to meet student needs.	1.b.1.1 The number of students performing at or above 60% will increase by 3% by the spring of 2004. The number of students performing below 60% will decrease by 3% by the spring of 2004.	1.b.1.1 a. Addison Wesley Mid-Year Test. b. CoGat Quantitative and ITBS math as indicators of both potential and achievement.	1.b.1.1 Pretests and chapter tests as well as daily scores and class participation.

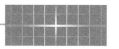
Sample B:

DISTRICT GOAL: IMPROVE STUDENT ACHIEVEMENT PK-12				
Goal Statement What is/are our school's goal area(s) to reach the district-wide goal?	**Implementation Strategies** What are our action steps we will take to reach our school's goal?	**Success Criteria/ Specific Outcomes** What <u>measurable results</u> do we expect for <u>students</u>?	**Data Collection Methods** How will we collect data to measure our progress towards the goal?	
			Baseline/Trend-line Data	Up-close Data
1.4 Improve reading for all students.	1.4.1 Develop three study groups to investigate reading strategies at the high school level. 1.4.2 Implement ideas from study groups. 1.4.3 Evaluate data.	1.4.1 ITEDs scores raised for students or use of a reading assessment to show reading growth.	1.4.1 ITED Testing.	
2.1 Improve student respect, active citizenship, and demonstration of good character.	2.1.1 Evaluate seminar and develop new ideas.	2.1.1 Student evaluations. 2.1.1 Improved student academic achievement.	2.1.1 Student surveys. 2.1.1 Grades.	
3.4 Improve student learning through communication and collaboration with families and the community.	2.1.2 Monitor, assess, and improve on presented lessons. Evaluate four-year seminar initiatives. 3.4a.1 Continue committee to review the National PTA Standards for Parent Involvement. 3.4b.1 Continue publication of newsletter. 3.4c.1 Develop student profiles for Futures Program.	3.4a.1 Action plan based on Standards. 3.4b.1 Increased parent involvement and volunteerism. 3.4c.1 Increased number of scholarship recipients.	3.4b.1 Futures Program data base. 3.4c.1 Reports from parents, students, and guidance counselor.	

Sample C:

DISTRICT GOAL: IMPROVE STUDENT ACHIEVEMENT PK-12				
Goal Statement What is/are our school's goal area(s) to reach the district-wide goal?	**Implementation Strategies** What are our action steps we will take to reach our school's goal?	**Success Criteria/ Specific Outcomes** What <u>measurable results</u> do we expect for <u>students</u>?	**Data Collection Methods** How will we collect data to measure our progress towards the goal?	
			Baseline/Trend-line Data	Up-close Data
1.1 Improve student performance in reading for understanding.	1.1.1 Provide in-services on reading strategies in content areas. 1.1.2 Provide IRBS reading scores to teams at beginning and middle of year to identify students not achieving one year's growth in reading comprehension. 1.1.3 Utilize problem solving stages to address students not achieving in reading areas.	1.1 Reduce for each subgroup the percentage of students performing at the low performance level as measured by the ITBS.	1.1 Low Performance Level of ITBS: Reading Program = 58% Special Education = 78% Regular Education = ??%	1.1.1 IRIs. Direct Instruction.
1.a2 Provide opportunities for reading for enjoyment.		1.a2.1 Students will participate in reading activities with teams responding at an increase of 25%. Student group will be formed with initial goal of six students (one from each team).	1.a2.1 Student participation and survey.	

Part 2:

Using the same quality criteria, rate the selection of Implementation Strategies on your own Action Planning Sheet using the scale of 1-5, where 1 = Minimally; 3 = To a large extent; 5 = Absolutely. When this is completed, make recommendations for amendments.

Quality Criteria	Your Action Plan
Relevance and appropriateness	
Drawn from the external data base	
Well-matched to identified internal needs	
Customized for local use	
Well-suited to flexible diagnostic application	
Applicable to sustained, systematic implementation	
Likely to have staff support and commitment	

Recommendations for amendments:

Part 3

a. Read Sample Action Planning Sheets D, E, and F that follow.

b. Using these samples, containing only the **Goal Statement** (column 1) and the **Success Criteria/Specific Outcomes** (column 4), complete each plan by adding **Data Collection Methods** (column 5) and **Implementation Strategies** (column 2).

Note: **Support Needs** (column 3) has been omitted for this exercise.

Sample D:

DISTRICT GOAL: IMPROVE STUDENT ACHIEVEMENT PK-12				
Goal Statement What is/are our school's goal area(s) to reach the district-wide goal?	**Implementation Strategies** What are our action steps we will take to reach our school's goal?	**Success Criteria/ Specific Outcomes** What <u>measurable results</u> do we expect for <u>students</u>?	**Data Collection Methods** How will we collect data to measure our progress towards the goal?	
			Baseline/Trend-line Data	Up-close Data
1.1 Students will become better problem solvers.		1.1 No more than 30% of our students in any designated subgroup will performance at the low performance level using ITBS building level achievement reports.		

Sample E:

DISTRICT GOAL: IMPROVE STUDENT ACHIEVEMENT PK-12				
Goal Statement What is/are our school's goal area(s) to reach the district-wide goal?	**Implementation Strategies** What are our action steps we will take to reach our school's goal?	**Success Criteria/ Specific Outcomes** What <u>measurable results</u> do we expect for <u>students</u>?	**Data Collection Methods** How will we collect data to measure our progress towards the goal?	
			Baseline/Trend-line Data	Up-close Data
3.1 Improve student character and citizenship through volunteerism.		3.1 There will be a 10% improvement on student survey questions related to respect between students and the need to support the community. There will be a 10% increase in participation in service related organizations.		

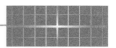

Sample F:

DISTRICT GOAL: IMPROVE STUDENT ACHIEVEMENT PK-12				
Goal Statement What is/are our school's goal area(s) to reach the district-wide goal?	**Implementation Strategies** What are our action steps we will take to reach our school's goal?	**Success Criteria/ Specific Outcomes** What <u>measurable results</u> do we expect for <u>students</u>?	**Data Collection Methods** How will we collect data to measure our progress towards the goal?	
			Baseline/Trend-line Data	Up-close Data
1.b To improve performance in reading of students with special needs.		1.b Students will achieve the following performance levels on district language arts assessment measures: ■ State-mandated test an average of one year on reading composite ■ Observation Survey 80% at or above grade level ■ District assessment 80% at or above 75%		

Action planning is ...

- ■ nothing without a SHARP, CLEAR FOCUS.

- ■ predicated on the notion that LESS IS MORE; it's a question of being PACKAGED FOR SUCCESS.

- ■ best tackled when the change is viewed as a MAJOR INVESTMENT in which the participants are SHAREHOLDERS wanting/needing to CAPITALIZE ON THEIR INVESTMENT. (It's a case of being COST-CONSCIOUS as well as CHANGE-CONSCIOUS.)

- ■ the BRIDGE between GOAL SETTING and IMPLEMENTATION. (Therefore, it makes no sense to separate the roles of planner and implementer. In order to maximize involvement, ownership, and commitment, they have to be one and the same.)

- ■ best done in participative, theme-related, interest-based TEAMS.

- ■ the time to build in and plan for MONITORING and EVALUATION by establishing SUCCESS CRITERIA/SPECIFIC OUTCOME INDICATORS.

- ■ exactly what it says. (It is the PLAN FOR ACTION [i.e., IMPLEMENTATION] and needs to be PRACTICAL, DOWN-TO-EARTH, and REALISTIC.)

What have you
learned so far?

What are you
continuing to
think about?

What are you
going to do
differently in
the future?

STAGE 5

Taking the Action

Overview

The school improvement process is often referred to as the school improvement planning process. This is something of a misnomer; while the overall process involves planning, the resulting plans also have to be implemented. Plans are necessary but not sufficient. Indeed, one of the dangers of quick-fire legislative changes at both federal and state levels is that schools and school districts are continually having to plan and then re-plan—without ever getting a chance to really give implementation the degree of attention it deserves.

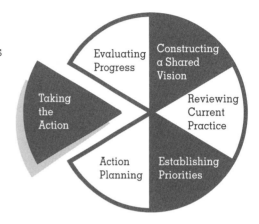

Despite its vital importance, when it comes to implementation, we border on being inexperienced beginners. Meanwhile, we remain virtually addicted to detailed planning. The harsh truth is that it's safer in the planning stage; planning by itself does not entail change. Indeed, when the author revisited a school that had produced the best of school improvement plans one year earlier, he found that implementation efforts were sadly lacking. When asked why, staff members responded by saying that they were so proud of their plan, yet felt paralyzed when it came to moving forward. That is where leadership and accountability, pressure and support, are vital ingredients of the school improvement process. School leaders have to create the kind of conditions that both prompt yet nurture their colleagues' change efforts. As Joyce and Showers (1982) have also pointed out, the more that staff training that includes guided practice and collegial coaching can be instituted, the more likely the participating teachers are to launch into classroom implementation.

By definition, this is the action stage; put simply, it is when the action plan is implemented. As this author has written previously (in Bellamy, Holly, and Sinisi, 1997):

> As the name implies, the action cycle is where things get done; this is where change occurs in the school. Change does not just happen, however. It is made to happen, and the steps in the action cycle—studying, planning, acting, and evaluating—help organize the effort required for real changes.

The action stage is uniquely different—for five reasons:

1. While the previous stages have all been "needs-based data-driven," it is during the action stage that this approach is used for change-making where it matters most—at the classroom level.

2. The action stage is composed of action cycles with a short time span. In the spirit of action research, these mini-cycles allow for the application of small-scale, highly focused and carefully planned interventions and the scrutinizing of their impact on student learning. In the light of these findings, modifications are made and another mini-cycle is mounted. Each of these mini-cycles might only take a matter of weeks to complete.

3. This action stage is also smaller in terms of the scale of involvement. What typifies this stage is the deployment of small work groups. These teams might be functional groups like grade-level teams in the elementary school, interdisciplinary teams in the middle school, and departmental teams in the high school, or they might be *ad hoc*, temporary problem-solving teams formed around a particular school goal. These are often referred to as action teams.

4. The locus of control shifts during the action stage. Those in the driver's seat are the work group members—the classroom practitioners. Because they are members of relatively small teams, their interests, concerns, and enthusiasms come to the fore. In addition, while they may share responsibility for a particular school goal, each team member might approach the work with a different strategy in mind. This need not take away from their team operation; they can still share and support each other's actions and reflections.

5. The action stage gets to the true purpose of school change: improving teaching and learning in classrooms across the school. What happens in the classroom during implementation is the acid test for any particular intervention. Does it work for this teacher, with these students, in this context? The action-researching teacher becomes intrigued with these questions.

During this stage of the school improvement process, therefore, change enters the world of the classroom—through the agency of action research as the process vehicle. Classroom action research will be described in depth in the third workbook in this series, *Engaging in Action Research*. Suffice it to say at this point that classroom action research—entered into collaboratively but with individual enthusiasms to the fore—is the mainstay of carefully engineered change efforts.

Calhoun (1999) would definitely agree. She has written extensively about action research in schools and its vital role within the implementation process. She makes four points that are crucial in this context:

■ The implementation process has to be supported by **time** for the kind of staff development that applies good learning theory. As part of their staff development, teachers implement new strategies to advance student performance related to the school's goal throughout the year.

■ At the same time, teachers need to regularly collect "up-close" data, data as close to the student performance as possible. For example, work samples could be collected and scrutinized on a weekly, bi-weekly, or monthly basis.

■ None of this will happen unless the principal and a core group of teacher leaders are fully engaged and are willing to use all they know to help everyone move forward. A school's level of implementation, she says, can be gauged by how engaged the principal is in modeling what is happening.

■ The more focused the change efforts are, the more likely they are to succeed. It is action research, she says, that helps us narrow the focus to broaden our effectiveness.

Some of the characteristics of action research are listed as follows (Holly, 1999):

■ data gathering by participants

■ learning progressively and publicly by doing—in a self-reflective spiral of planning, acting, observing, reflecting, and re-planning

■ self-reflection, self-assessment, and self-management by autonomous and responsible persons and groups

■ reflection by the practitioner

■ collaboration among members of the group as a supportive but critical community

■ above all, the personalization of the change process—in line with the organization's action plans

This process of personalizing the school's change agenda is enhanced by the use of the commitments sheet such as the "Personal Classroom Projects" example included on the following page.

PERSONAL CLASSROOM PROJECTS
In the light of your team's Action Plan, what emerges as an appropriate Focus Area for your personal classroom? What is your personal goal?
What is the District and/or School Goal that your personal project addresses? What action steps are suggested to you from the original Action Plan?
Given your interest in this topic, what external data (regarding potential strategies to use) do you have available to you?
What baseline data do you have available to you to indicate the current status in your topic area?
What strategies/interventions are you going to use to achieve the desired results?

Taking the Action
Task 1: Focusing on Local Implementation Efforts

Purpose: To reflect on the extent and quality of local implementation efforts.

Grouping: Work with your Learning Team.

Directions: With your team, reflect on the contents of the Overview by answering these two questions:

1. In what ways do your current change practices match the problems (concerning too much planning, too little implementation) described previously? In what ways do they not match?

2. In what ways could your current change practices be strengthened by following the advice given in the Overview? What positive differences would this make in your change practices?

What else is different about the Action Stage?

During the Action Stage of the school improvement process, there is

- increased accountability for individual and teams of teachers

- more awareness of the importance of effective teamwork

- the recognition that all the decentralized individual and small-group endeavors need to be supported, coordinated, orchestrated, and aligned with the centralized plans of the local school system by the members of the School Improvement Team

Increased Accountability

Commitments sheets like the one included above are an indication that, with the decentralization of classroom implementation efforts, comes more professional responsibility and accountability. In his fascinating study entitled *Flow: The Psychology of Optimal Experiences*, Csikszentmihalyi (1990) argues that growth involves becoming more complex. Complexity, he says, is the result of two broad psychological processes: *differentiation* and *integration*. Differentiation implies a movement towards uniqueness and separating oneself from others, while integration refers to its opposite—a union with others beyond the self. A complex self, he concludes, is one that succeeds in combining these opposite tendencies. Indeed, without integration, a differentiated system would be a confusing mess. And it's exactly the same with the change process: there has to be increased differentiation *and* integration—simultaneously. This is why action teams and their action plans (sub-sets of the school's action plans) become so important. Teamwork becomes the departure point for differentiation and the safe harbor of integration. It is chiefly in teams that increased responsibility and accountability are located.

In Dubuque Schools, it has been discovered that written and agreed upon team commitments sheets can be a powerful force for both differentiation and integration. Besides explaining the expectations of the administration, action teams, and action team chairpersons, these commitments sheets establish reporting procedures, basic tasks to be accomplished, and progress reviews to be undertaken—in terms of those students who have met (or not met) the success criteria. Sample sheets are contained on the following pages.

PROGRESS REVIEW

Subject ______________________ Grade Level ______________________

Success Criteria (student-based) ______________________________________

Baseline Assessment ______________

Total Number of Students [ ]

Number of Students Meeting Criteria* [ ]
*Success criteria—refer to building plan

Percentage of Students Meeting Criteria [ ]

Students who met or exceeded criteria
(Please list)

1. ______________________
2. ______________________
3. ______________________
4. ______________________
5. ______________________
6. ______________________
7. ______________________
8. ______________________
9. ______________________
10. ______________________
11. ______________________
12. ______________________
13. ______________________

Students who did not meet criteria
(Please list)

1. ______________________
2. ______________________
3. ______________________
4. ______________________
5. ______________________
6. ______________________
7. ______________________
8. ______________________
9. ______________________
10. ______________________
11. ______________________
12. ______________________
13. ______________________

_____ School

Comprehensive School Improvement Plan

School Year:_____

Action Team Quarterly Update to the Site Council

Action Team: _____

Chairperson: _____

Reporting Period: _____

Report Due Dates:
■ November 22
■ January 20
■ March 20
■ End-of-Year Summary and Evaluation

Please submit each update to the site council on or before the due date.

■ What has been the focus and what were the related activities of this action team during this time period?

  ■ Trying to figure out how to assess the school math goal.

  ■ Discussing different ways this might be accomplished.

■ What has been accomplished during this time period?

  ■ Staff meeting to try to help answer questions about concepts covered and not covered at all grade levels.

  ■ Information gathered to help determine how to establish baseline.

■ What are your plans for the next time period?

  ■ Inform teachers of using/revising mid-year test to give every year after completing first half of math text.

147

> ### Sample
> ### Classroom Action Research Process Worksheet
> ### Irving School
> ### School Year: _____

Teachers,

Use this worksheet to plan your classroom action research. Questions 1-6 can be answered now. Question 7 should be done at the end of the research. Remember that the research should be based on the school plan. You can use data that you are currently collecting, such as BRI or STAR, as success data. Use the November 21 staff meeting time to complete this worksheet. Please turn this sheet into office by Wednesday, November 21.

1. Define the problem: *The students in the bottom reading group have low comprehension.*

2. Specify a classroom target goal: *Students will pass the Macmillan comprehension part of the test with 70 % accuracy.*

3. List the school plan goal that coincides with the classroom goal: *1.1—Provide additional programs/services for students with special needs in reading.*

4. Make a plan to reach that goal: *Students will take the STAR test and participate in Accelerated Reader to help increase reading comprehension.*

5. Determine success data: *Students will improve their reading comprehension performance by one year on the STAR test or pass Macmillan comprehension test with 70 % accuracy.*

6. Implement the plan and collect data—start date: *Start 12/3/XX*

7. Reflect on results: _____

_____

_____

_____

_____

_____

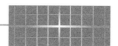

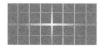 Taking the Action
Task 2: Examining Accountability

<u>Purpose:</u> To investigate how educators are currently held accountable for making change happen.

<u>Grouping:</u> Work individually and then meet with your Learning Team to discuss.

<u>Directions:</u> Describe how teams and individual teachers are held accountable for making changes happen in your local situation.

In the opinion of your group, are these procedures sufficient? Why or why not? What else might be needed?

Team Effectiveness

The success of school improvement efforts lies in the success of the teams created to shepherd the process. School Planning Teams are largely for initiating, coordinating, and supporting the process. It is the goal-based action teams that must bear the brunt of the work—and be accountable for their efforts. It is essential, therefore, that action teams are able to work effectively—by using group process strategies, such as those described in the **Group Process Guide**—and are asked to make regular progress reports to the members of the School Improvement Team/Site Council.

The idea of keeping team records through the use of a team log was suggested by Munger (1989). She sees the responsibility for documenting progress as an essential part of the accountability process. An example of her suggested log is included below.

TEAM LOG

Date:_____ Team Goal/Focus:_____ Starting/Ending Time:_____

Facilitator:_____ Collaboration Time:_____

Phase III Time:_____ Recorder:_____ Other Time:_____

Team Members: _____

1) Team Building Idea/Warm up: _____

2) Review Ground Rules/Focus on: _____

3) Agenda:

Order of Priority	Agenda Items	Process	Process Key	Time (in minutes)	Roles/Assigned to:
			■ Dialogue ■ Round Table Discussion		Facilitator:
			■ Program Solving ■ Pairs		Secondary Facilitator:
			■ Cooperative Processing ■ Priority Weighting/Voting		Time Keeper:
			■ Individual Work ■ Presentation/Sharing		Recorder:
					Scribe:

TEAM LOG *(continued)*

4) Reflection:

    a. Summary of activities/accomplishments: _____

_____

_____

(Key words to use: generated, planned, decided, explained, developed, listened, shared)

    b. What were your learnings? _____

    c. What ways could you extend these learnings to your classroom for the benefit of student learning? _____

_____

    d. Will you be able to measure/document these benefits? How? _____

_____

    e. Processing of team functioning (Descriptive feedback +/-)

       + What did we do well today? _____

       - What could we have done better? _____

5) Focus for next time:

    a. Questions/Issues/Topics to put on the agenda: _____

_____

    b. Agenda to be distributed by: Name: _____ Date: _____

    c. Individual assignments: _____

_____

    d. Materials needed: _____

    e. Meeting Place: _____ Date/Time: _____

151

Recording Progress in Data

The members of each action team should be concerned with showing progress—in their respective goal area—over time. Each team, therefore, should have a data collection plan. An example is included below.

Goal Area _____

Success Criteria	Baseline Data	Up-close Data	Trend-line Data

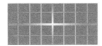 Taking the Action
Task 3: Evaluating Action Team Effectiveness

<u>Purpose:</u> To evaluate the effectiveness of the action teams.

<u>Grouping:</u> Work individually and then meet with your Learning Team to discuss.

<u>Directions:</u> How would you rate the effectiveness of your action teams—or their equivalent? Score each of the elements below on a 1–5 scale with 5 being "High" and 1 being "Low."

Rating:

_____ Clearly defined roles and responsibilities

_____ Self-management

_____ Appropriate membership

_____ Meeting schedule that works

_____ Effective group process

_____ Recording procedures

_____ Data collection

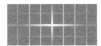 Taking the Action
Task 4: Identifying Team Strengths and Challenges

<u>Purpose:</u> To summarize the strengths of the action teams and the ways in which they need to improve.

<u>Grouping:</u> Work individually and then meet with your Learning Team to discuss.

<u>Directions:</u> List on the next page the strengths and challenges that emerge from the assessment of your action teams.

Strengths	Challenges

At the Organizational Level

While the action teams and the teachers conducting action research are bearing the brunt of the implementation work, the School Improvement Team has the responsibility of ensuring that a.) not more than one important initiative is at the implementation stage each year and b.) regular progress reports are received "from the front line." The paperwork used for this second purpose in Dubuque and Sioux City Schools is reproduced on the next few pages.

THE LIFE CYCLE OF A SCHOOL IMPROVEMENT INITIATIVE			
Year	**Stage**	**Code**	**Task Example**
1	Study and Planning	S	■ Examine external data (best practices, research, literature)
2	Early Implementation	E	■ Initial implementation efforts ■ Action research projects ■ Small-scale (pilots) or whole school ■ End-of-year progress review and modifications
3	Implementation	I	■ Full involvement ■ Action research projects ■ Monitor and evaluate ■ Modifications
4	Maintenance	M	■ Continuing implementation to the point of internalization ■ Ongoing monitoring and evaluating

TIMELINE				
'01–'02	**'02–'03**	**'03–'04**	**'04–'05**	**'05–'06**
S	E	I	M	
	S	E	I	M
		S	E	I
			S	E

DATA COLLECTION PLAN

Goal: _____

Baseline Data	Up-close Data	Trend-line Data
Methods used:	Methods used:	Methods used:
Results:	Results:	Results:
Emerging issues:	Emerging issues:	Emerging issues:

DUBUQUE CSD: SPRING

I. Reviewing Progress:

CSIP Long Range Goal: _____

Annual Improvement Goal: _____

Success Indicators (Grade Level or Course Specific Benchmarks)	Assessment Methods	Results	Implications for the Future

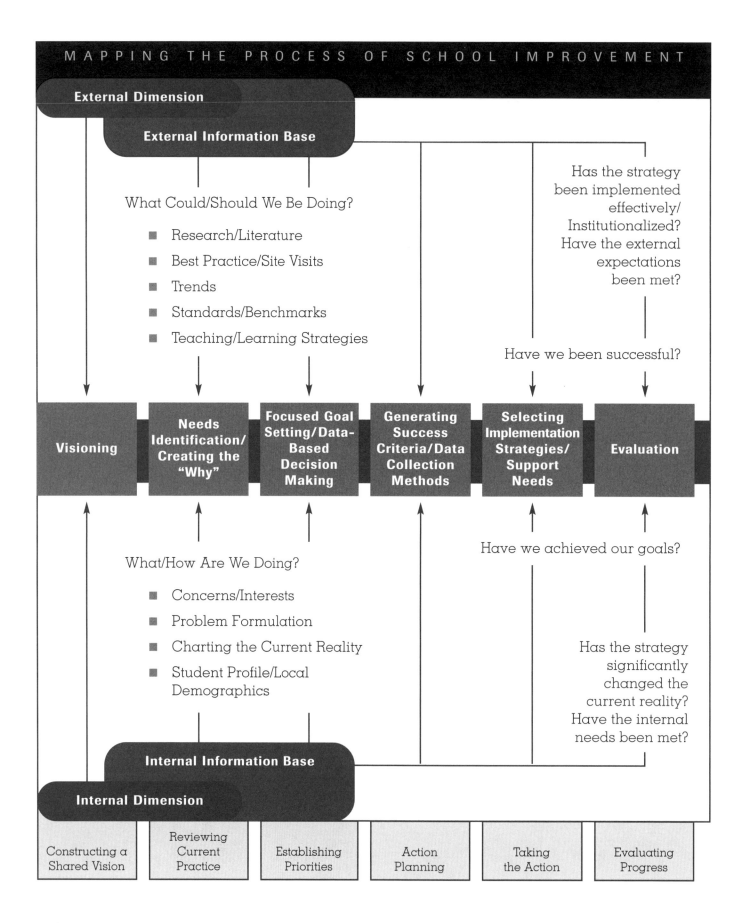

MAPPING THE PROCESS OF SCHOOL IMPROVEMENT

External Dimension

External Information Base

What Could/Should We Be Doing?

- Research/Literature
- Best Practice/Site Visits
- Trends
- Standards/Benchmarks
- Teaching/Learning Strategies

Has the strategy been implemented effectively/ Institutionalized? Have the external expectations been met?

Have we been successful?

Visioning	Needs Identification/ Creating the "Why"	Focused Goal Setting/Data-Based Decision Making	Generating Success Criteria/Data Collection Methods	Selecting Implementation Strategies/ Support Needs	Evaluation

What/How Are We Doing?

- Concerns/Interests
- Problem Formulation
- Charting the Current Reality
- Student Profile/Local Demographics

Have we achieved our goals?

Has the strategy significantly changed the current reality? Have the internal needs been met?

Internal Information Base

Internal Dimension

Constructing a Shared Vision	Reviewing Current Practice	Establishing Priorities	Action Planning	Taking the Action	Evaluating Progress

SIOUX CITY COMMUNITY SCHOOLS
BUILDING SCHOOL IMPROVEMENT PLANNING

The following format will be used in the Spring of _____ when
reporting your building school improvement plan.

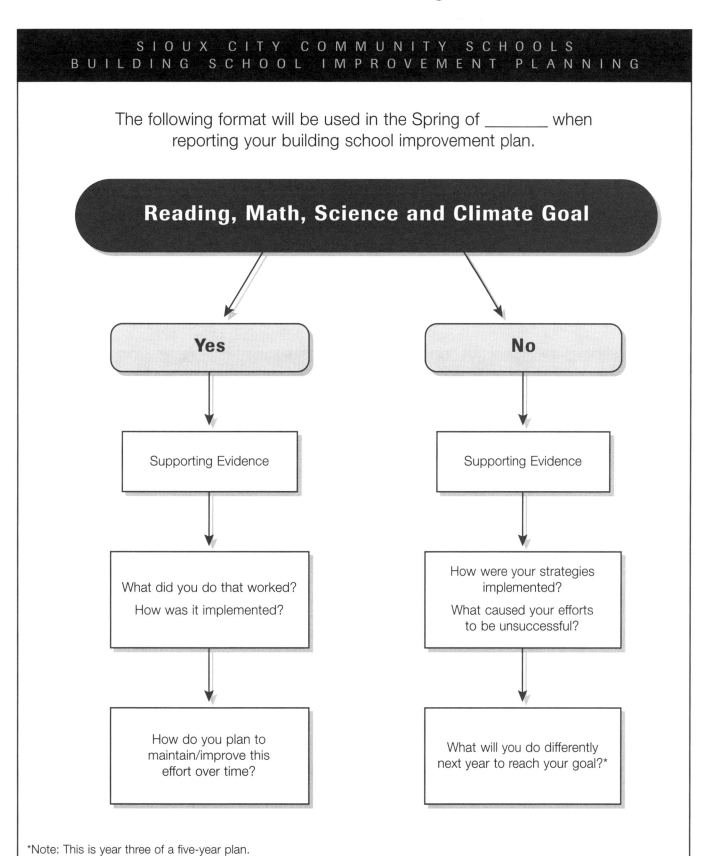

Reading, Math, Science and Climate Goal

Yes

Supporting Evidence

What did you do that worked?

How was it implemented?

How do you plan to
maintain/improve this
effort over time?

No

Supporting Evidence

How were your strategies
implemented?

What caused your efforts
to be unsuccessful?

What will you do differently
next year to reach your goal?*

*Note: This is year three of a five-year plan.

SPRING _____ : REPORTING ON PROGRESS OF SCHOOL IMPROVEMENT PLANS

Goal: _____

Supporting Evidence

Data Sources	Progress Made

Implementation

How were your strategies implemented?

What did you do that worked?

What did not work?

What caused your efforts to be unsuccessful?

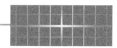

Future Implications:

How do you plan to maintain/improve this effort over time?

What will you do differently next year to reach your goal?

How will your five-year plan be updated?

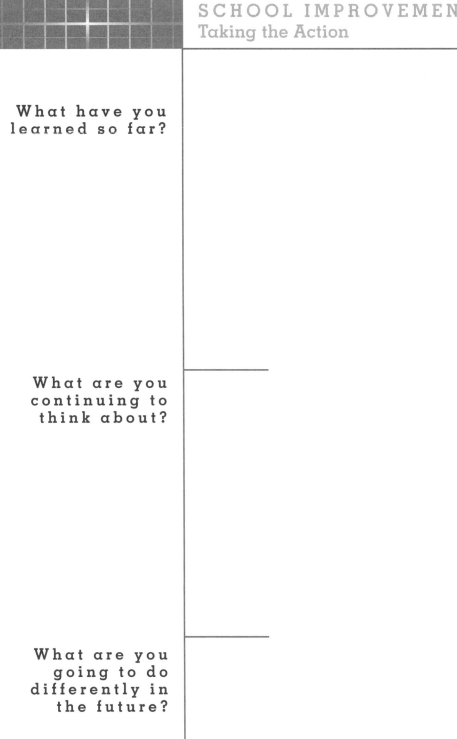

What have you learned so far?

What are you continuing to think about?

What are you going to do differently in the future?

Stage 6

Evaluating Progress

Overview

It is crucial to monitor and evaluate progress over time—at the organizational level. While classroom action research directly helps participants in their change efforts, what is required here is data feedback concerning progress of the entire school improvement plan. Monitoring is more of a formative activity and can occur on an annual basis; evaluating progress is a more summative, long-term activity and should be conducted on, for example, a tri-annual basis.

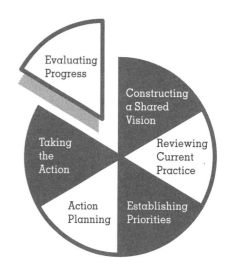

Evaluating progress entails the following:

- a summative review of the progress made toward the school's vision

- measuring growth against the performance levels contained in the original baseline data

- quantifying the extent of goal (and success criteria) achievement

- judging the quality and quantity of the accomplishments on three levels:

  - the impact on student learning

  - the impact on instructional practice

  - the impact on school climate

 Evaluating Progress ▪ Task 1: Analyzing Local Applications of School Improvement Plans

<u>Purpose:</u> To ascertain what is currently done locally to monitor and evaluate the application of school improvement plans.

<u>Grouping:</u> Work with your Learning Team.

<u>Directions:</u> In your team, discuss what is done currently in your school or district to monitor and evaluate progress over time. Does it work? Is it done frequently enough?

Case Materials

In Iowa, districts such as Dubuque and Sioux City use an annual review and reporting form (see the previous section). In Dubuque, action team members are asked to submit their reports to the school's site council by the end of April—for collation, review, and re-planning (if necessary). The accompanying examples of completed report forms were prepared by Mary Lange, and used as simulated training materials.

Evaluating Progress
Task 2: Strengthening Local Efforts

Purpose: To consider how these exemplar materials could be used to strengthen local efforts to monitor and evaluate the long-term application of school improvement plans.

Grouping: Meet with your Learning Team.

Directions: Looking at the materials (presented on the following pages), discuss how your school/school district could benefit from this approach to reviewing and reporting progress.

PROGRESS REVIEW

DCSD Goal #1: Improve student performance in reading for understanding and enjoyment.

School Goal(s)	Success Indicators (Intended Results)	Assessment Methods	Results	Implications for the Future
Provide a strong Language Arts program that allows students to develop to their fullest potential.	80% of students will achieve 70% or higher on the end-of-the-year grade level Macmillan tests.	End-of-the-year grade level Macmillan tests.	80% of students scored 79% or higher.	The majority of students are achieving appropriately with the current instruction. Identify those for whom this instructional approach has not assisted in reaching this level of achievement (the red alerts) and identify additional interventions. For next plan, increase to 83% or level to 72%.
Improve the level of performance in reading and writing.	65% of students will score a 6, 7, or 8 on the holistically scored district writing assessment.	Curriculum-based assessment.	63% achieved this level.	Continue with current interventions, set similar indicators for next plan with additional interventions where applicable.
	80% of students will read 2-4 hours a month independently.	Teacher log survey.	Incomplete information.	Collaboratively establish firm timelines for teacher logs and identify responsibilities for reporting. Maintain current success indicators.
Reduce the number and percentage of students performing at the "low" level.	A higher percent (10%?) of students taking the ITEDs exam within their class; higher test composites by grade level, 9th and 11th.	ITED analysis.	Increased by 20% the number of students taking the test. Composite scores in reading increased by 2.5%.	Set success indicator for next year for 95% participation in ITEDs. Set success indicators with percent of students achieving at a specific level. Conduct an item analysis of reading comprehension scores; identify students in need of intervention and appropriate activities.
Improve reading for understanding in content areas.	Decrease by 10% the percentage of students with difficulty reading in the content areas.	(Teacher observational checklist.)	Anecdotal evidence that teachers needed further skills and tools in order to complete the observational checklists to their satisfaction. Additional requests from teachers for preparation in instruction of reading in content areas.	Success indicators for next year's plan should include additional assessment(s) of higher order reading skills. Improvement levels will not be possible until baseline data is collected; therefore, success indicators might be that baseline data will identify % of students achieving at the 70% level on the assessment.

PROGRESS REVIEW

DCSD Goal #2: Improve student performance in mathematics in the areas of problem solving, math reasoning, measurement, computation, and concept attainment.

School Goal(s)	Success Indicators (Intended Results)	Assessment Methods	Results	Implications for the Future
Increase student proficiency in math.	The # of students performing at or above grade level will increase by 5% by the spring of 2004; # of students performing below grade level will decrease by 5% by the spring of 2004.	ITBS/ITED scores, unit tests.	The # of students performing at or above grade level increased by 1% and the # of students performing below grade level did not decrease.	Maintain the earlier success indicator, but use two additional assessment methods. Based on these assessment results, disaggregate and conduct item analyses to identify which students are continuing to have problems with which specific skills.
	Math students will be pretested prior to unit instruction using end-of-chapter tests. Students who score 85% or above will be taught the skills missed and will be given alternate (not additional) materials and/or activities during the remainder of the unit.	Unit test scores and alternative curriculum will be kept on the Advanced Math Record Cards.	The students who were identified in this group and provided the instruction described, increased math scores on all the unit tests by at least one year.	Maintain this process as a Continuing School Improvement Initiative (Parking Lot) and instead address a reading goal because our students' reading scores were disappointing.
Improve student performance in the areas of mathematics, computation, and problems/ data interpretation.	80% of students in the Extended Day Math Tutoring Program will make a minimum of one year's growth on all math sub-tests.	ITBS.	79% of students showed a minimum of one year's growth.	Maintain current success indicators, disaggregate the 21% who have not achieved at the desired level and use two other assessment methods to analyze.

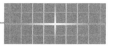
PROGRESS REVIEW

DCSD Goal #3: Nurture and support a safe learning environment based on mutual respect, active citizenship, and demonstration of good character.

School Goal(s)	Success Indicators (Intended Results)	Assessment Methods	Results	Implications for the Future
To establish a climate in which there is ■ respect for one another ■ a caring attitude ■ a strong sense of responsibility ■ demonstration of appropriate behavior.	There will be fewer than 5 Office Interventions per child per school year.	Office Intervention records.	There were no more than 3 Office Interventions per child during the school year for all but 10 of the students.	The next success indicators should address those students who were not able to maintain the earlier identified standard. Additional assessments of the goal should be identified and used to monitor the behaviors of those 10 students.
Building climate that is calm and respectful.	10 additional students will benefit from the attention of caring adult mentors (resulting in fewer absences, increased success with school work and social situations).	Track successful recruitment of area retirees; students, mentors, and teachers evaluate program results.	8 additional students participated. Program was evaluated as a success.	Maintain current success indicators. Survey potential mentors to determine if there are other issues that need to be resolved (e.g., scheduling complications, lack of information about the impact of the program).
Create a culture of mutual respect.	At least 75% of the student body will be acknowledged through the rewards/incentive systems.	Tracking by team of teachers in collateral time, shared during early dismissal.	78% of the student body was thus acknowledged.	Celebrate the success. Identify the students who were not included and plot data about those students. Determine any correlation between assessment results and these results.
There will be a decrease in violent exchanges.	Increase by 10% the use of the mediation program.	Monitor the number of harassment reports and mediations.	Use was increased by 25%.	Celebrate the success. Have students, staff, and parents surveyed to identify need for and means of expanding the program. Include in next success indicators other assessment methods (e.g., surveys related to sense of safety).

PROGRESS REVIEW

DCSD Goal #4: Strengthen communication and collaboration within the school system and with families and the community to support student learning.

School Goal(s)	Success Indicators (Intended Results)	Assessment Methods	Results	Implications for the Future
Strengthen communication and collaboration with families and the community to support student learning.	80% of all students at all grade levels will return a parent-signed reading log on a weekly or a monthly basis.	Teacher survey.	75% of students returned reading log on weekly basis.	Maintain current success indicator. Identify students who did not return the reading log and track the reasons, through student interviews, calls to parents, etc. Triangulate with 2 reading assessments and provide documentation that will be addressed for those who do not yet see the value.
Develop and increase involvement of community members, parents, and business partners.	40% of volunteers invited will attend an appreciation celebration.	The event will happen as scheduled and numbers of attendees logged.	More than 40% of invitees attended!	The appreciation ceremony should be continued. Follow-up surveys could be used to assess perceptions of the stakeholders in necessity of their being involved.
Strengthen communication and collaboration with families and the community to support student learning.	100% of students experiencing academic or behavioral difficulties will have had parents or guardians contacted.	Parent log documentation	Although not all parents of these students had phones available, teachers made some sort of contact with each of them.	This goal and its success indicator needs to be continued with results of the contacts being documented and tracked, then triangulated with the data that identified the students as having behavioral or academic difficulties. Where appropriate, problem solving should be used.

Evaluating the School Improvement Planning Process

Guiding Questions for Self-Assessment

1. Content

   a. Are the goals well focused on important, worthwhile areas?

   b. Are the implementation strategies sufficiently rigorous and research-based (i.e., grounded in the external knowledge base)?

   c. Are the success indicators focused on *student learning results* that are *quantifiable*?

2. Process

   a. Are all elements of the district format for the Comprehensive School Improvement Plan (CSIP) included?

   b. Is the plan, and therefore are the goals, sufficiently needs-based, data-driven?

   c. Does the current plan reflect that we are in a five-year planning sequence?

   d. What is your school doing to implement this plan at the classroom level?

3. Relationships

   a. Is the plan the result of broad-based involvement (i.e., have goal-based Action Teams been involved)?

   b. What is the depth of commitment to the plan?

   c. Has the plan been discussed with all key stakeholders?

Using the ten questions listed above, the following self-assessment instrument was designed to assess the overall school improvement planning process of Holly and Lange (2001).

A SELF-ASSESSMENT OF THE SCHOOL IMPROVEMENT PROCESS

			Your Rating
1.	**Content**	The goals are well-focused on important, worthwhile areas.	
		The implementation strategies are sufficiently rigorous and research-based (i.e., grounded in the external knowledge base).	
		The success indicators are focused on student learning results that are quantifiable.	
2.	**Process**	All elements of the district format for the CSIP are included.	
		The plans, and therefore, the goals, are sufficiently needs-based, data-driven.	
		The current plan reflects that you are in a five-year planning sequence.	
		Your school shows evidence of implementing this plan at the classroom level.	
3.	**Relationships**	The plan is the result of broad-based involvement (i.e., goal-based Action Teams have been involved).	
		There is a depth of commitment to the plan.	
		The plan has been discussed with all key stakeholders.	

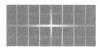

Evaluating Progress
Task 3: Evaluating the School Improvement Process

<u>Purpose:</u> To use the assessment instrument to evaluate the quality of the school improvement process.

<u>Grouping:</u> Work individually and then meet with your Learning Team to share.

<u>Directions:</u> Using the Self-Assessment chart shown above, rate the quality of your school improvement process on each of these statements using a 1-5 scale with 1 being "Strongly Disagree" to 5 being "Strongly Agree."

An alternative progress review survey is included on the following pages.

SCHOOL IMPROVEMENT: PROGRESS REVIEW

Use a 1–5 scale to indicate your answers to the following questions.

1= WHAT?   2 = LEARNING   3 = IN PROGRESS

4 = PROGRESS EVIDENT   5 = ABSOLUTELY!

Rating	Progress Review
	1. Are your goals aligned with the district's vision?
	2. Are your goals sufficiently grounded in internal data?
	3. Are your goals focused on student learning?
	4. Do your goals integrate various school improvement initiatives (e.g., Success4, School-to-Work)?
	5. Are the goals supported by detailed action plans, which include staff development activities?
	6. Are these action plans being implemented at the classroom level?
	7. Are your implementation strategies grounded in an external research base?
	8. Do you have success criteria for monitoring your progress?
	9. How will you gather evidence to show your success?
	10. Do you have mechanisms in place to share your success with your wider public?
	11. Do students have meaningful ways to be actively involved in school improvement efforts?
	12. Have students been trained in group processing techniques (e.g., conflict resolution, team problem solving)?
	13. Have students been encouraged to take leadership roles in the community?
	14. Are students involved in assessing their own learning progress (e.g., student-led conferences)?
	15. Do students and parents understand learning expectations at each grade level?
	16. Do you have multiple assessments for monitoring and reporting on student progress?
	17. Are assessment results used for informing decision making at the classroom, building, and district levels?
	18. Are the assessments connected to your standards and benchmarks?
	19. Have all staff members received training in the use of a variety of assessment methods?
	20. Do you have a management system for recording assessment data?
	21. Do you have a "School Improvement Team," which represents the School Board, administration, teachers, staff, and students?

Continued

SCHOOL IMPROVEMENT: PROGRESS REVIEW (cont'd)	

Use a 1–5 scale to indicate your answers to the following questions.

1= WHAT?　2 = LEARNING　3 = IN PROGRESS

4 = PROGRESS EVIDENT　5 = ABSOLUTELY!

Rating	Progress Review
	22. Do you have an Advisory Team that represents all local stakeholder groups?
	23. Is building leadership supportive of school improvement efforts?
	24. Is central office supportive of school improvement efforts?
	25. Are potential candidates for leadership development identified and supported in your district?

Please indicate your position in the district:

☐ Teacher　　　　　☐ Staff Member　　　☐ Student

☐ Building Administrator　☐ Board Member　　☐ Community Member

☐ Central Office Administrator　☐ Parent　　　☐ Other

Reflective Participant Feedback

A vastly under-used means of monitoring and evaluating progress is reflective participant feedback. Included below is an example received from Cynthia Nelson, formerly a teacher at Bryant School in Dubuque and a participant in the original "Framing School Improvement" training program. Writing in 1997, she said:

> 'Its purpose is to explore avenues to reduce the load in order to be able to do the right things well...to be more accountable for less.' As the introductory page in the manual for this workshop, the words above seemed sound, but as with many workshops a question that came to mind was: "Can this actually be done so simply, or are the presenters, in fact, giving us more work, more ideas, more time consuming buzz words for which we must be accountable?"...
>
> In my twenty years in education many initiatives have come and most have remained—with more piled on top of those previously introduced. The site-based decision-making model advocated in these

workshops shows us how to take what we are doing, throw out the chaff, and keep what is needed for institutional excellence. The major focus I internalized was the need for **data to drive all decisions**. So many times an idea became the model of the day simply because someone had read an article about a successful school which found new ways to impart knowledge to its clients. The thought that all achievement for students comes from an organized plan conceived with forethought and data was not exactly new, but this workshop brought such common sense attitudes forward in my thinking. I was especially pleased to note that data should be obtained from many sources, not just a parent survey or ITBS tests. As an Expeditionary Learning school, we must obtain data on the efficacy of our E.L. stance. We discussed this along with all modes of data collection and found that we do have much of this data in hand. Now the task is to centralize this data into a usable form to help us write future plans.

To see that in education "less is more" is not a radical thought but one which had not been practiced in my previous experience....The presenter's attitude and experience gave the participants permission to find the things which are important to the particular setting and to seek excellence in that setting. Demographically different sites are now able to find what fits their needs and to write a plan, which assures them of a focused path to success. Also apparent was the need to continue these plans over a reasonable length of time so that in their maturity the ideas can become practice and be internalized.... This means a concerted effort must be made by all involved to see the vision, understand the focus, and be 'in for the long haul.'

As we write a three-year site plan, we must reflect on past practices as a foundation of the plan. There is not a vacuum that this plan is being written to fill. It is grounded in what we have done very well and know we will continue to do....The evaluation of the plan, assessing the ramifications of practices in previously written goals, is integral to its success. So many times a piece is kept for unknown reasons, maybe simply because it is there. With this training, we know that we can take out what is no longer needed, pausing to note the data for this decision, and add or rework pieces which data show us are needed.

I found that through the insights I gained from this workshop that I was monitoring our plan more closely....There is a need to make all stakeholders feel this ownership of the plan so that they too will monitor its path...

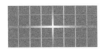

Evaluating Progress
Task 4: Reflecting on Positive Messages

<u>Purpose:</u> To reflect on the messages emerging from this case study material.

<u>Grouping:</u> Work individually.

<u>Directions:</u> Using the space below, respond to the following question.

Given these reflective comments, what are the positive messages for the organizers of the training and the school improvement process in Dubuque?

Another Dubuque teacher, Susan Merritt, also reflected on her role in the school improvement process, again, in 1997:

> This has been a tremendous year for my own personal growth. I believe that being a part of the site council and a part of the training will stay with me for life. I have a new appreciation for what a site council does and how important the job is. I also have a newfound appreciation and respect for school principals and administrators.
>
> I am currently working on the evaluation for the Audubon School Plan. The task is laborious but very gratifying. The task of compiling artifacts is arduous. Through this process we have devised a school profile form that we will begin using next school year. The school profile will also help me in my current job at Audubon. As the at-risk strategist for the school, I use much of the information for reports to the state. These reports are data-driven. We have included the following: enrollment; socio-economic status; attendance and tardies; class size; student referrals to health and social services; special programs; test data; reading proficiency levels; number of computers; and number of staff.
>
> We have also decided to keep an artifact folder for each grade level. This will help with the evaluation process that seems to loom in May and June....This planning is a very serious and deliberate process that cannot be completed easily. Site planning that is done effectively should impact our school and children for life.

Evaluating Progress
Task 5: Providing Reflective Feedback

<u>Purpose:</u> To provide participants with the opportunity to reflect on their personal involvement in local school improvement activities.

<u>Grouping:</u> Work individually.

<u>Directions:</u> Working individually, reflect on your school's current involvement in school improvement activities. What would you say to the organizers in your district? Present your thoughts in the space provided below. What works well? What might they do differently and why?

<u>My Reflective Feedback</u>

Some Concluding Thoughts

The CREATE model has now been fully explained. Its cyclical nature, its reliance on data-driven growth, and its emphasis on continuous improvement make it a near relative of the ideas promoted by W. Edwards Deming and Total Quality Management (TQM). As Bonstingl (1992) has explained:

> Deming encourages educators to create school environments in which strong relationships of mutual respect and trust replace fear, suspicion, and division; and in which leadership from administrators and policymakers empowers students and teachers (as front-line workers of the school) to make continuous improvements in the work they do together.

Echoing Senge (1990) and Holly and Southworth (1989), Bonstingl sees the developing school as a growing, continuously improving, and optimizing learning organization. CREATE is the process vehicle for such a school.

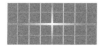

Evaluating Progress
Task 6: Charting the Course

<u>Purpose:</u> To identify and prioritize specific actions related to a defined area of opportunity for implementing the school improvement process.

<u>Grouping:</u> Work individually and then meet as a group.

<u>Directions:</u> Working individually (and then collating all the individual responses), now is the time to reflect on the opportunities, the required actions related to these opportunities, and the challenges still facing your school/school district when it comes to implementing the school improvement process.

To facilitate the identification and prioritization of action items, the Nominal Group Technique (NGT) is recommended. According to the *Pocket Tools for Education* (1996), the NGT is a structured group process used to help make decisions concerning the choice of actions for improvement. It involves the following steps:

1. State the defined area of opportunity.

2. Silently generate action items related to the defined opportunity, such as, "Establish a time for grade-level teams to meet to discuss the new spelling program."

3. Share and record action items—using the Go Round technique.

4. Discuss each item on the list.

5. Establish criteria for voting.

6. Conduct a preliminary vote by ranking the various items.

7. Add the scores to determine the high priority actions (*see below).

Rankings	Action Items
3–3–2–3–2	1. Establish a weekly training program for teachers.
1–2–1	2. Set up a mentoring program.
1	3. Subscribe to professional journals for teachers.
2–3–1–3	4. Write a manual with examples of lessons plans that integrate objectives.
	5. Establish an expert in each building.
2–1	6. Establish an expert in each grade level.
	7. Train all new teachers to integrate objectives.
	8. Develop a new lesson planning sheet that includes hints for integration of test objectives.

* *Item #1 chosen as best action idea.*

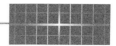

About the Author

Peter Holly is the author of the PATHWISE: *Data-Driven School Improvement* series. Having been a teacher, administrator, researcher, and school improvement consultant in the United Kingdom, since 1990 he has worked solely with schools and school districts in the United States. He was one of the lead consultants for Schools for the Twenty-First Century in Washington State, the National Education Association's (NEA) Learning Lab project, and the New Iowa Schools initiative. Currently, he is an independent school improvement consultant working with school systems mainly in the Midwest. In helping school systems become more change-oriented and data-driven, he uses many of the materials to be found in this workbook.

Notes

180

References

Argyris, C. and Schon, D. (1978). *Organizational Learning: A Theory of Action Perspective.* Reading, Mass: Addison-Wesley.

Bellamy, G. T., Holly, P., and Sinisi, R. (1997). *The Cycles of School Improvement.* National Staff Development Council.

Berman, P., and McLaughlin, M.W. (1976). Implementation of Educational Innovations. *Educational Forum. 40*, 345–370.

Bernhardt, V. L. (1998). *Data Analysis for Comprehensive Schoolwide Improvement.* Larchmont, NY: Eye on Education.

Bonstingl, J. J. (1992). *Schools of Quality: An Introduction to Total Quality Management in Education.* Alexandria, VA: Association for Supervision and Curriculum Development.

Calhoun, E. (1990). *Some Common Data Analysis Questions.* Training Materials.

Calhoun, E. (1999). The Singular Power of One Goal. *Journal of Staff Development;* National Staff Development Council. Winter, 54–58.

Champion, R. (2002). Taking Measure: Map Out Evaluation Goals. *Journal of Staff Development*, 23, 4.

Collins, J. (1996). Aligning Action and Values. in Hesselbein, F. and Cohen, P. M. (eds.). *Leader to Leader.* The Drucker Foundation. San Francisco, CA: Jossey-Bass.

Covey, S. (1989). *Seven Habits of Highly Effective People.* New York: Simon and Schuster.

Csikszentmihalyi, M. (1990). *Flow: The Psychology of Optimal Experience.* New York, Harper and Row.

Festinger, L. (1954). *A Theory of Cognitive Dissonance.* Stanford, CA: Stanford.

Fullan, M. (1982). *The Meaning of Educational Change.* New York: Teachers College Press.

Fullan, M. (1987). *Managing Curriculum Change* in *Curriculum at the Crossroads.* London: SCDC.

Garmston, R.J. and Wellman, B. (1999). *The Adaptive School. A Sourcebook for Developing Collaborative Groups.* Norwood, MA: C. Gordon.

Garmston, R.J. (2002). Group Wise. *Journal of Staff Development. 23*(3), 74–75.

Goodlad, J. (1984). *A Place Called School.* New York: McGraw-Hill.

Guskey, T. R. (1990). Integrating Innovations. *Educational Leadership.* February, 47(5).

Hampel, R. (1995). The Micropolitics of RE: Learning. *School Leadership.* November, 5(6), 597–616.

Hatch, T. (2002). When Improvement Programs Collide. *Phi Delta Kappan*, *83*(8), 626–635.

Holcomb, E. L. (1999). *Getting Excited about Data*. Thousand Oaks, CA: Corwin Press.

Holly, P. (1990). *The Developing School*. Training Materials. National Education Association (NEA) Workshops.

Holly, P. (1996). Too Many Solutions for Too Few Problems. *Reflections Newsletter*. New Iowa Schools Development Corporation (NISDC).

Holly, P. (1999). *Introducing Action Research*. Training Materials. The Learning Group.

Holly, P. (2003). *Case Studies in School Leadership: Keys to a Successful Principalship*. Princeton, NJ: Educational Testing Service.

Holly, P. and Sagor, R. (1989). *Effective Schools Inventory*. Training Materials.

Holly, P. and Southworth, G. (1989). *The Developing School*. London: The Falmer Press.

Holly, P. and Lange, M. (2001). *Ten Questions to Ask of School Improvement*. Training Materials. The Learning Group.

Johnson, D.W. and Johnson, F.P. (2000). *Joining Together. Group Theory and Group Skills*. Boston: Allyn and Bacon.

Joyce, B. and Showers, B. (1982). The Coaching of Teaching. *Educational Leadership*, *40*(1), 4–10.

Joyce, B., Wolf, J., and Calhoun, E. (1993). *The Self-Renewing School*. Alexandria, VA: Association for Supervision and Curriculum Development.

Lo, Ya-Yu and Cartledge, G. (2001–2). Using Office Referral Data to Improve School Discipline. *Streamlined Seminar*. Winter, *20*(2). National Association of Elementary School Principals.

Munger, L. (1989). *Study Group Log*. Training Materials.

Murphy, C. (1987). *Effective Groups*. Training Materials.

Murphy, C. (1995). Whole-Faculty Study Groups: Doing the Seemingly Undoable. *Journal of Staff Development*. Summer, *16*(3).

Naisbitt, J. (1982). *Megatrends. Ten New Directions Transforming Our Lives*. New York: Warner Books.

Naisbitt, J. and Aburdene, P. (1990). *Megatrends 2000*. New York: Morrow.

National Inservice Network. (1980). *Needs Assessment for Inservice Education: Building Local Programs*. Bloomington, Indiana. August.

North Central Association (NCA). (2000). *Developing the School Profile. A Handbook for Schools.* NCA Commission on Schools. Tempe, AZ: Arizona State University.

Patterson, J. L., Purkey, S. C., and Parker, J. V. (1986). *Productive School Systems for a Non-Rational World.* Alexandria, VA: Association for Supervision and Curriculum Development.

Peck, S. (1987). *The Different Drum: Community Making and Peace.* New York. Simon & Schuster.

PQ Systems. (1996). *Pocket Tools for Education.* Miamisburg, OH.

Public Agenda. (1999). *Kids These Days 1999: What Americans Really Think About the Next Generation.* New York.

Richardson, Joan (1996). If You Don't Know Where You're Going, How Will You Know When You Arrive? *School Team Innovator.* September. National Staff Development Council.

Schmoker, M. (1996). *Results: The Key to Continuous School Improvement.* Alexandria, VA: Association for Supervision and Curriculum Development.

Schon, D. (1983). *The Reflective Practitioner.* London: Temple Smith.

Senge, P. (1990). *The Fifth Discipline.* New York: Doubleday.

Sparks, D. (1994). A Paradigm Shift in Staff Development. *Journal of Staff Development.* Fall, 15(4).

Weisbord, M. and Janoff, S. (1995). *Future Search. An Action Guide to Finding Common Ground in Organizations and Communities.* San Francisco, CA: Berrett-Koehler.

Notes

184

Notes

Notes

188

Notes

190

Notes

192

These materials are being sponsored by the Teaching and Learning Division of Educational Testing Service (ETS), a not for profit organization. One of the division's goals is to serve teachers' professional development needs by providing products and services that identify, assess, and advance good teaching from initial preparation through advanced practice.

Educational
Testing Service
Teaching and Learning
Division

Our mission is to help advance quality and equity in education by providing fair and valid assessments, research and related services. Our products and services measure knowledge and skills, promote learning and performance, and support education and professional development for all people worldwide.

We welcome your comments and feedback.

Email address: professionaldevelopment@ets.org

Professional Development Group
Teaching and Learning Division
Educational Testing Service, MS 18-D
Princeton, New Jersey 08541